TWENTY-FIVE DAYS

of

Christmas

TWENTY-FIVE DAYS

of

Christmas

PREPARING FOR THE KING

DR. TEDDY OTT

TATE PUBLISHING
AND ENTERPRISES, LLC

This book is designed to provide accurate and authoritative information with regard to the subject matter covered. This information is given with the understanding that neither the author nor Tate Publishing, LLC is engaged in rendering legal, professional advice. Since the details of your situation are fact dependent, you should additionally seek the services of a competent professional.

The opinions expressed by the author are not necessarily those of Tate Publishing, LLC.

Published by Tate Publishing & Enterprises, LLC
127 E. Trade Center Terrace | Mustang, Oklahoma 73064 USA
1.888.361.9473 | www.tatepublishing.com

Tate Publishing is committed to excellence in the publishing industry. The company reflects the philosophy established by the founders, based on Psalm 68:11,
"The Lord gave the word and great was the company of those who published it."

Book design copyright © 2015 by Tate Publishing, LLC. All rights reserved.
Cover design by Joshua Rafols
Interior design by Mary Jean Archival

Published in the United States of America

ISBN: 978-1-68254-135-7
Religion / Holidays / Christmas & Advent
15.10.09

Contents

Prophesy Fulfilled

Jesus was from the beginning:

> In the beginning was the Word, and the Word was
> with God, and the Word was God. He was in the
> beginning with God. All things were made through
> him, and without him was not anything made that
> was made. In him was life, and the life was the light
> of men. The light shines in the darkness, and the
> darkness has not overcome it.
>
> —John 1:1–5 (esv)

Jesus, the coming Messiah is the promised seed of Abraham.

Old Testament prophecy: "I will surely bless you, and I will surely multiply your offspring as the stars of heaven and as the sand that is on the seashore. And your offspring shall possess the gate of his enemies, and in your offspring shall all the nations of the earth be blessed, because you have obeyed my voice" (Gen. 22:17–18, esv).

New Testament fulfillment: "The book of the genealogy of Jesus Christ, the son of David, the son of Abraham" (Matt. 1:1, ESV).

Jesus was promised through Isaac.

Old Testament prophecy: "But God said to Abraham, 'Be not displeased because of the boy and because of your slave woman. Whatever Sarah says to you, do as she tells you, for through Isaac shall your offspring be named" (Gen. 21:12, ESV).

New Testament fulfillment: "The son of Jacob, the son of Isaac, the son of Abraham…" (Luke 3:34, ESV).

Jesus would be born out of the tribe of Judah.

Old Testament prophecy: "But you, O Bethlehem Ephrathah, who are too little to be among the clans of Judah, from you shall come forth for me one who is to be ruler in Israel, whose coming forth is from of old, from ancient days" (Mic. 5:2, ESV).

New Testament fulfillment: "The son of Amminadab, the son of Admin, the son of Arni, the son of Hezron, the son of Perez, the son of Judah…" (Luke 3:33, ESV).

Jesus would be born in the family of Jesse.
Old Testament prophecy:

> There shall come forth a shoot from the stump of Jesse, and a branch from his roots shall bear fruit. And the Spirit of the LORD shall rest upon him, the Spirit

of wisdom and understanding, the Spirit of counsel and might, the Spirit of knowledge and the fear of the LORD. And his delight shall be in the fear of the LORD. He shall not judge by what his eyes see, or decide disputes by what his ears hear, but with righteousness he shall judge the poor, and decide with equity for the meek of the earth; and he shall strike the earth with the rod of his mouth, and with the breath of his lips he shall kill the wicked. Righteousness shall be the belt of his waist, and faithfulness the belt of his loins. The wolf shall dwell with the lamb, and the leopard shall lie down with the young goat, and the calf and the lion and the fattened calf together; and a little child shall lead them. The cow and the bear shall graze; their young shall lie down together; and the lion shall eat straw like the ox. The nursing child shall play over the hole of the cobra, and the weaned child shall put his hand on the adder's den. They shall not hurt or destroy in all my holy mountain; for the earth shall be full of the knowledge of the LORD as the waters cover the sea. In that day the root of Jesse, who shall stand as a signal for the peoples—of him shall the nations inquire, and his resting place shall be glorious. In that day the Lord will extend his hand yet a second time to recover the remnant that remains of his people, from Assyria, from Egypt, from Pathros, from Cush, from Elam, from Shinar, from Hamath, and from the coastlands of the sea. He will raise a signal for the nations and will assemble the banished of Israel, and gather the dispersed of Judah from the four corners of the earth. The jealousy of Ephraim shall depart, and those who harass Judah shall be cut off; Ephraim shall not be jealous of Judah, and Judah shall not harass Ephraim. But they shall swoop down on the shoulder of the Philistines in the west, and together they shall plunder the people of the east. They shall put out their hand against Edom and Moab, and the Ammonites shall obey them. And the LORD will utterly destroy the tongue of the Sea of Egypt, and will wave his hand over the River with his scorching breath, and strike it into seven channels, and he will lead people across in sandals. And there will be a highway from Assyria for the remnant that remains of his people, as there was for Israel when they came up from the land of Egypt. (Isa. 11, ESV)

New Testament fulfillment: "The son of Jesse, the son of Obed, the son of Boaz, the son of Sala, the son of Nahshon" (Luke 3:32, ESV).

Jesus would be born in the house of King David.
Old Testament prophecy:

Behold, the days are coming, declares the LORD, when I will raise up for David a righteous Branch, and he shall reign as king and deal wisely, and shall execute justice and righteousness in the land. In his days Judah will be saved, and Israel will dwell securely. And this is the name by which he will be called: "The LORD is our righteousness." (Jer. 23:5–6, ESV)

New Testament fulfillment: "The son of Melea, the son of Menna, the son of Mattatha, the son of Nathan, the son of David" (Luke 3:31, ESV).

Jesus would be born in Bethlehem.

Old Testament prophecy: "But you, O Bethlehem Ephrathah, who are too little to be among the clans of Judah, from you shall come forth for me one who is to be ruler in Israel, whose coming forth is from of old, from ancient days" (Mic. 5:2, ESV).

New Testament fulfillment:

> And Joseph also went up from Galilee, from the town of Nazareth, to Judea, to the city of David, which is called Bethlehem, because he was of the house and lineage of David, to be registered with Mary, his betrothed, who was with child. And while they were there, the time came for her to give birth. (Luke 2:4–6, ESV)

Jesus would be born of a virgin.

Old Testament prophecy: "Therefore the Lord himself will give you a sign. Behold, the virgin shall conceive and bear a son, and shall call his name Immanuel" (Isa. 7:14, ESV).

New Testament fulfillment: "Now the birth of Jesus Christ took place in this way. When his mother Mary had been betrothed to Joseph, before they came together she was found to be with child from the Holy Spirit" (Matt. 1:18, ESV).

Jesus would be worshipped and presented gifts by kings.

Old Testament prophecy: "May the kings of Tarshish and of the coastlands render him tribute; may the kings of Sheba and Seba bring gifts!" (Ps. 72:10, ESV).

New Testament fulfillment: "And going into the house they saw the child with Mary his mother, and they fell down and worshiped him. Then, opening their treasures, they offered him gifts, gold and frankincense and myrrh" (Matt. 2:11, ESV).

Jesus would be worshipped by shepherds.

Old Testament prophecy: "May desert tribes bow down before him, and his enemies lick the dust!" (Ps. 72:9, ESV).

New Testament fulfillment: And in the same region there were shepherds out in the field, keeping watch over their flock by night. And an angel of the Lord appeared to them, and the glory of the Lord shone around them, and they were filled with great fear. And the angel said to them, "Fear not, for behold, I bring you good news of great joy that will be for all the people. For unto you is born this day in the city of David a Savior, who is Christ the Lord. And this will be a sign for you: you will find a baby wrapped in swaddling cloths and lying in a manger." And suddenly there was with the angel a multitude of the heavenly host praising God and saying, "Glory to God in the highest, and on earth peace among those with whom he is pleased!" When the angels went away from them into heaven, the shepherds said to one another, "Let us go over to Bethlehem and see this thing that has happened, which the Lord has made known to us" (Luke 2:8–15, ESV).

There would be weeping for the children.

Old Testament prophecy: "Thus says the LORD: 'A voice is heard in Ramah, lamentation and bitter weeping. Rachel is weeping for her children; she refuses to be comforted for her children, because they are no more" (Jer. 31:15, ESV).

New Testament prophecy: "Then Herod, when he saw that he had been tricked by the wise men, became furious, and he sent and killed all the male children in Bethlehem and in all that region who were two years old or under, according to the time that he had ascertained from the wise men" (Matt. 2:16, ESV).

Mary and Joseph would flee to Egypt.

Old Testament prophecy: "When Israel was a child, I loved him, and out of Egypt I called my son" (Hosea 11:1, ESV).

Comments: The nation of Israel was God's firstborn "son"—this is a figurative use of the word. But the firstborn "son" of pharaoh was a literal son. So there are two different meanings of the word *son* in the passage in Exodus. Hosea refers to the first when he refers to Israel as God's "son." Matthew sees that Hosea's words that were written for the nation of Israel using the figure of a son find their fullest meaning in the experience of Jesus the Son as He is "called" out of Egypt to go to the land of Israel. We therefore have two levels of meaning for Hosea 11:1—the primary reference is Israel in the Exodus, but the ultimate application is to the fulfillment of the exodus from Egypt in the person of Jesus. Matthew is not simply connecting Jesus's return from Egypt with the exodus of Israel from Egypt; he is connecting all that was involved with that exodus with Jesus.

New Testament fulfillment: "Now when the wise-men had departed, behold, an angel of the Lord appeared to Joseph in a dream and said, 'Rise, take the child and his mother, and flee to Egypt, and remain there until I tell you, for Herod is about to search for the child, to destroy him'" (Matt. 2:13–14).

Jesus was to be called Lord.
Old Testament prophecy: "The LORD says to my Lord: 'Sit at my right hand, until I make your enemies your footstool'" (Ps. 110:1, esv).

New Testament fulfillment: "For unto you is born this day in the city of David a Savior, who is Christ the Lord" (Luke 2:11, esv).

Jesus is the Son of God.

Old Testament prophecy: "I will tell of the decree: The LORD said to me, "You are my Son; today I have begotten you" (Ps. 2:7, ESV).

New Testament fulfillment: "And behold, a voice from heaven said, 'This is my beloved Son, with whom I am well pleased'" (Matt. 3:17, ESV). "And the Holy Spirit descended on him in bodily form, like a dove; and a voice came from heaven, 'You are my beloved Son; with you I am well pleased'" (Luke 3:22, ESV). "And a voice came from heaven, 'You are my beloved Son; with you I am well pleased'" (Mark 1:11, ESV).

The Preparation Begins

As it is written in Isaiah the prophet, "Behold, I send
my messenger before your face, who will prepare your
way, the voice of one crying in the wilderness: 'Prepare
the way of the Lord, make his paths straight.'"

—Mark 1:2–3 (ESV)

John the Baptist prepares the way.

Old Testament prophecy: "A voice is calling, 'Clear the
way for the Lord [YHWH] 1 in the wilderness; make smooth
in the desert a highway for our God" (Isa. 40:3).

"'Behold, I am going to send My messenger, and he will
clear the way before Me. And the Lord [Adonai], whom you
seek, will suddenly come to His temple; and the messenger

of the covenant, in whom you delight, behold, He is coming, says the Lord [YHWH] of hosts" (Mal. 3:1).

New Testament fulfillment: "There was a man sent from God, whose name was John. He came as a witness, to bear witness about the light, that all might believe through him. He was not the light, but came to bear witness about the light. The true light, which gives light to everyone, was coming into the world" (John 1:6–9, esv).

Don't Miss Christmas!

Now after Jesus was born in Bethlehem of Judea in the days of Herod the king, behold, wise men from the east came to Jerusalem, saying, "Where is he who has been born king of the Jews? For we saw his star when it rose and have come to worship him." When Herod the king heard this, he was troubled, and all Jerusalem with him; and assembling all the chief priests and scribes of the people, he inquired of them where the Christ was to be born. They told him, "In Bethlehem of Judea, for so it is written by the prophet:

"'And you, O Bethlehem, in the land of Judah,
are by no means least among the rulers of Judah;
for from you shall come a ruler
who will shepherd my people Israel.'"

Then Herod summoned the wise men secretly and ascertained from them what time the star had appeared. And he sent them to Bethlehem, saying, "Go and search diligently for the child, and when you have found him, bring me word, that I too may come and worship him."

—Matthew 2:1–8 (ESV)

You know Christmas is almost here when...

There are more pine needles on your carpet than on your tree. The credit card is smoked along with the turkey and the ham. *It's a Wonderful Life* has been shown for the ten times in a row. A shopping trip to the mall and back is more challenging than the Indianapolis 500. The Salvation Army bell ringers are standing outside every store. You have to pull an all-nighter on Christmas Eve because of the words "Some Assembly Required," or your Christmas list is written in black while your checkbook balance is written in red.

Did you know that most people miss out on Christmas every year? That may sound rather silly when we are drowned in the sea of Christmas advertisements during the holidays. How can anyone miss Christmas? Yet millions will miss Christmas this year. There at least five groups of people who missed that first Christmas, and those people will miss Christmas this year.

The following people have a No Vacancy sign hanging in the doorway of their lives:

The Innkeeper

That first Christmas, it was the innkeeper who missed Christmas. The innkeeper missed the first Christmas because he was preoccupied. The town was crowded. There was no indication that he was hostile or even unsympathetic to this pregnant woman. He was just too busy and had no room for the Savior. We can become so busy with activities that sinful that we miss the true meaning of Christmas (and the Savior). So many people don't have room for Christ in their Christmas. The innkeeper missed the first Christmas by refusing to let Jesus be born in his house. Similarly, so many people miss Christmas by not letting Jesus be born in their hearts.

Herod

Unlike the innkeeper, this man was not ignorant as to who Jesus was. He pretended he wanted to worship Jesus, by he was really fearful of letting Jesus be Lord. If Jesus became Lord, it would ruin his career and change everything. There are lots of people who are like Herod. They won't allow Jesus to be Lord because he would interfere with the following:

- career
- position
- plans
- lifestyle

Warning! When Jesus becomes Lord of your life, He will change everything!

The Religious Group

Matthew 2:4 says,

> And when he had gathered all the chief priests and scribes of the people together, he demanded of them

> where Christ should be born. And they said unto him,
> In Bethlehem of Judaea: for thus it is written by the
> prophet, And thou Bethlehem, in the land of Judea, art
> not the least among the princes of Judea: for out of thee
> shall come a Governor, that shall rule my people Israel.

The chief priests and scribes knew exactly where Jesus Christ, the Messiah, was to be born. These were the theologians, the minds, the brains, the religious elite of Israel. They knew Scripture well enough to quote Micah 5:2, which prophesied that Messiah would be born in Bethlehem. Yet they missed Christmas! Even though they outwardly prayed for the Messiah to come and deliver them from the Romans, they never even bothered traveling a few miles south to Bethlehem to see if the Messiah had indeed been born. Why do the religious often miss Jesus? Because they don't care to seek Him out. These religious leaders thought, *Surely when the Messiah comes, He won't pass us by. We're the ones that fast twice a day and give tithes of all we have and keep tradition. Surely we're the crowd He'll come to first.* They were self-righteous. They had the "I'm all right the way I am" attitude. This is an attitude that will cause people to miss Christmas year after year. Jesus's ministry was to people who had a problem called sin and knew it.

The Romans

They were ruling Israel and were in control. Roman soldiers must have been scattered all over Bethlehem to keep order as the great crowds of people gathered for the census, yet they did not recognize who Jesus was because of their idolatry. These types of people miss Christmas year after year as because they are too busy worshipping other gods (self, material things, etc.).

The People of Bethlehem and Nazareth

Finally and perhaps the saddest of all who missed Christmas were the hometown folks. The people who resided where Jesus would grow up. Jesus was born in Bethlehem; He grew up in Nazareth and lived His perfect life before all the people who lived there, yet they completely overlooked Him. The people of Bethlehem missed the Savior because they were sleeping. They missed Jesus because they thought they knew the way it should all be (they had it all planned out). Jesus had lived in Nazareth all His life and then makes the proclamation that He is the Messiah. What was their reaction? The people who knew Jesus best, those with whom He would grow up and lived among would try to kill Him. The people of Nazareth, who knew Him better than anyone, had no idea who He really was! What was their problem? Familiarity was the problem. They knew Him too well. They knew Him so well that they couldn't believe He was anyone special. Familiarity often strangles conviction. Perhaps the most tragic sin of all is the unbelief of a man, woman, or young person who has heard all the sermons, has sat through all the Bible teachings, knows the Christmas story back to front, but rejects Jesus as

Lord. There is no Gospel, no good news for such a person, because he or she already knows but rejects the only truth that sets them free.

Don't miss Christmas this year. Not one person ever missed Jesus because they were watching for Him. Will you turn on your vacancy sign this Christmas and watch and wait for Jesus's appearing?

Be Ready!

Therefore you also must be ready, for the Son of
Man is coming at an hour you do not expect.

—Matthew 24:44 (ESV)

Be watchful, stand firm in the faith, act like men, be
strong.

—1 Corinthians 16:13 (ESV)

Advent is a season in the Christian year that lasts for about
four weeks. It begins four Sundays before Christmas and
ends on Christmas Eve. Very similar to the way many see
Christmas. Many begin putting up our Christmas decorations
around Thanksgiving in preparation for Christmas. For
some, however, the season of Christmas actually begins on

Christmas Eve and lasts for twelve days, ending on January 6, but that is not really the case for Christians because for us, the Christmas season is a time to prepare for the birth of Jesus. We know Jesus was indeed born on that first Christmas morning, coming as the promised Messiah. So now we celebrate this season of His birth in anticipation of His second coming, His return for us. In Advent, we're reminded as individuals of how much we need a Savior, to look forward to our Savior's second coming and to prepare for His return as we celebrate Christmas. So the celebration of Christmas is a time for us to prepare for the coming of the King. "Therefore you also must be ready, for the Son of Man is coming at an hour you do not expect" (Matt. 24:44, ESV). Sure, we should be preparing every single day, but this time of year is set aside to remind us of this truth.

The word *advent* comes from the Latin word *adventus*, which means "coming" or "visit." Therefore, in this season, we are to keep in mind both *advents* of Christ, the first in Bethlehem and the second yet to come.

Is the Christmas season a time of preparing for the coming of the Lord for you and your family? Or has it become too commercialized? I fear that for the follower of Jesus, the redeemed, the church, we have moved from celebrating the relationship that Jesus brought to us on that Christmas morn to making it a religious activity where we go through the motions, sing the songs, and attend our candlelight services, and even go so far as making Christmas a business or marketing too for our own gain. I pray that as we step into this Christmas season that we remember the Savior, celebrate the Messiah, cherish and build upon our relationship with Him, and become prepared for the return of the King of Kings and Lord of Lords. "Watch therefore, for you know neither the day nor the hour" (Matt. 25:13, ESV).

> *Lord, help us to build up on our relationship*
> *with You this season in such a way that we are*
> *preparing daily for Your return for us. Amen.*

Dressed and Standing
at the Door!

Beware of the Leaven of the Pharisees

In the meantime, when so many thousands of the people had gathered together that they were trampling one another, he began to say to his disciples first, "Beware of the leaven of the Pharisees, which is hypocrisy. Nothing is covered up that will not be revealed, or hidden that will not be known. Therefore whatever you have said in the dark shall be heard in the light, and what you have whispered in private rooms shall be proclaimed on the housetops.

Have No Fear

"I tell you, my friends, do not fear those who kill the body, and after that have nothing more that they can do. But I will warn you whom to fear: fear him who,

after he has killed, has authority to cast into hell. Yes,
I tell you, fear him! Are not five sparrows sold for two
pennies? And not one of them is forgotten before God.
Why, even the hairs of your head are all numbered.
Fear not; you are of more value than many sparrows.

Acknowledge Christ before Men

"And I tell you, everyone who acknowledges me before men,
the Son of Man also will acknowledge before the angels of
God, but the one who denies me before men will be denied
before the angels of God. And everyone who speaks a word
against the Son of Man will be forgiven, but the one who
blasphemes against the Holy Spirit will not be forgiven. And
when they bring you before the synagogues and the rulers
and the authorities, do not be anxious about how you should
defend yourself or what you should say, for the Holy Spirit
will teach you in that very hour what you ought to say."

The Parable of the Rich Fool

Someone in the crowd said to him, "Teacher, tell my
brother to divide the inheritance with me." But he said to
him, "Man, who made me a judge or arbitrator over you?"
And he said to them, "Take care, and be on your guard
against all covetousness, for one's life does not consist in
the abundance of his possessions." And he told them a
parable, saying, "The land of a rich man produced plentifully,
and he thought to himself, 'What shall I do, for I have
nowhere to store my crops?' And he said, 'I will do this: I
will tear down my barns and build larger ones, and there I

will store all my grain and my goods. And I will say to my soul, "Soul, you have ample goods laid up for many years; relax, eat, drink, be merry."' But God said to him, 'Fool! This night your soul is required of you, and the things you have prepared, whose will they be?' So is the one who lays up treasure for himself and is not rich toward God."

Do Not Be Anxious

And he said to his disciples, "Therefore I tell you, do not be anxious about your life, what you will eat, nor about your body, what you will put on. For life is more than food, and the body more than clothing. Consider the ravens: they neither sow nor reap, they have neither storehouse nor barn, and yet God feeds them. Of how much more value are you than the birds! And which of you by being anxious can add a single hour to his span of life? If then you are not able to do as small a thing as that, why are you anxious about the rest? Consider the lilies, how they grow: they neither toil nor spin, yet I tell you, even Solomon in all his glory was not arrayed like one of these. But if God so clothes the grass, which is alive in the field today, and tomorrow is thrown into the oven, how much more will he clothe you, O you of little faith! And do not seek what you are to eat and what you are to drink, nor be worried. For all the nations of the world seek after these things, and your Father knows that you need them. Instead, seek his kingdom, and these things will be added to you.

"Fear not, little flock, for it is your Father's good pleasure to give you the kingdom. Sell your possessions, and give to the needy. Provide yourselves with moneybags that do

not grow old, with a treasure in the heavens that does not
fail, where no thief approaches and no moth destroys. For
where your treasure is, there will your heart be also.

—Luke 12:1–34 (esv)

We have discussed how the first week of Advent and this time
of year reminds us to be ready for Jesus's return for us. The
second week teaches us to help prepare the way in anticipation
of Jesus's return. The third week of Advent is to help us to
recognize and convey the joy that the closeness of Christ's
return brings and the joy for the increased closeness of our
relationship, our personal relationship, with Him. The fourth
week of Advent is about sharing the Gospel. It is about telling
of the events that immediately preceded the birth of Jesus, and
that He is coming again, not as the Savior of the world but
as the final Judge. When He does, He will bless the faithful
servants, and the unfaithful servants will come into judgment.

Today we will continue this first week of our twenty-five
days of Christmas, preparing for the coming of our Savior. So
how do we prepare? I believe that Jesus gave us clear instruction
in His Word. We will see these instructions clearly as we pay
close attention to what Jesus says to His disciples. Jesus gave the
disciples five warnings. He had already warned them to avoid
hypocrisy (Luke 12:1–12) and to guard against greed and worry
(Luke 12:13–34). Now He is warning them to seek first the
kingdom of God. Jesus was telling them that as they seek first
the kingdom of God, they will be preparing for His return.

Jesus gets really specific on how to seek His kingdom in preparing for His return as He said,

> Stay dressed for action and keep your lamps burning, and be like men who are waiting for their master to come home from the wedding feast, so that they may open the door to him at once when he comes and knocks. Blessed are those servants whom the master finds awake when he comes. Truly, I say to you, he will dress himself for service and have them recline at table, and he will come and serve them. If he comes in the second watch, or in the third, and finds them awake, blessed are those servants! But know this, that if the master of the house had known at what hour the thief was coming, he would not have left his house to be broken into. You also must be ready, for the Son of Man is coming at an hour you do not expect. (Luke 12:35–40, ESV)

There are several things that we must talk about in relation to being prepared and seeking His kingdom, so we will touch on the first two today. We are to keep alert and we are to keep watch. Jesus says, "Stay dressed for action and keep your lamps burning, and be like men who are waiting for their master to come home."(Luke 12:35, ESV). As stewards, we are responsible to the Master for everything that is going on in our life. We are responsible for a well-run household. This means that we are faithful stewards who are willing to fulfill the will of our Master no matter what comes our way. Within our household, everyone must know that with faithfulness comes blessings, but unfaithfulness brings punishment. Jesus is returning as the King of Kings when He returns, and so we must be prepared. In preparing for the first Christmas people were preparing for the coming of the Messiah, and every Christmas since His ascension we should have been preparing for the King of Kings, the Righteous, True, and Holy Judge.

Now within the nation of Israel, the household and the stewards would have been the Pharisees and Sadducees, and the servants would have been the common people who sought to worship God. Today, the household stewards and slaves would be represented by the elders, pastors, deacons, and members of a local Christian church. Can you see our Lord and Savior Jesus Christ standing before us in the teachable moment of this Christmas season saying, "Stay dressed and be alert"? Can you hear the tremendous consequences that our choice will have in His voice? Our choice at His return to stay dressed and alert will bring blessing to the faithful, but the choice to do the opposite is to be unprepared and go on living a worldly life to the fullest, which will bring judgment to the unfaithful.

Lord, help us to stay dressed and alert by being good stewards of all that you have provided at all times. Lord, help us to seek first Your kingdom and Your righteousness this season. Amen!

DAY 3

Leave the Light On!

"Stay dressed for action and keep your lamps burning, and be like men who are waiting for their master to come home from the wedding feast, so that they may open the door to him at once when he comes and knocks. Blessed are those servants whom the master finds awake when he comes."

—Luke 12:35–37 (ESV)

We have been talking about the fact that the first week of Advent is about preparing for Christ. We said that though Jesus came in a manger on that first Christmas, He will be coming as Judge when He returns for us. Therefore, the first week of every Christmas season since His ascension should remind us about being prepared for His return. Make no mistake, we are not to simply be reminded that we are to be prepared for His return once or twice a year, but instead, being prepared for His return is a daily way of life for all those who truly trust in Him.

Remember Jesus's words in Luke 12—we are to be "dressed in readiness" at all times. Jesus gave the disciples a very familiar picture from that culture. Where the master had gone away to a wedding feast for several days, but then the time came for him to return. So the chief servant called all the others in the house and informed them that they were to tuck up their robes, stand by the door, and be ready so that when the master knocked, the door would be opened immediately, and when he entered, he would find his house in order and servants ready to serve him. We too are to be ready at all times this way.

Remember when Jesus was to be born? Only very few were prepared for the arrival of the Messiah. Only Mary and Joseph really responded quickly and adequately. When the angel told them of Jesus's arrival, they immediately opened their hearts to Him. Sure, there were a few shepherds and wise men who would respond after His birth, but they were not prepared as they should have been. Think about how long that God through the prophets and men like Moses, Jacob, Abraham, Joseph, and David had been telling them to be prepared. Since His people were not ready for His arrival the first time in Luke 12, Jesus is warning His disciples to be prepared for His second coming. By the way, if you are a follower of Christ, you are a disciple of Christ. Are you ready?

Just as He called His disciples of old, Jesus is calling His people, His church, to keep their lamps lit at all times and be ready. We said yesterday that the way we stay dressed and alert is to seek His kingdom first at all times. That is the way we keep our lamp lit and our light shining, isn't it? Seeking His kingdom first allows the Holy Spirit to keep our lamps filled with oil. When Jesus returns, He wants to find all His disciples shining as "the light of the world" (Matt. 5:14). He has set us aside so that by the power of the Holy Spirit (symbolized by the oil), we might keep the light of Jesus's character and the hope of His message of salvation shining through our lives and into the darkened hearts and minds of every unbeliever around us, resulting in redemption. This should be how we prepare every day until He returns again.

Jesus told his disciples to stand by the front door and wait. Doesn't it seem amazing to you that Jesus was looking past the cross to His resurrection, and His ascension to His second coming, wanting us to be prepared?

Are you so alert for the return of Jesus that you would immediately open the door, usher Him into your home, and have Him look around and find everything in order because you were ready? Are you alert and ready this Christmas season?

*Lord, help us to be dressed and ready, and we ask
that You help keep our lamps filled with oil and lit
at all times as we await Your return. Lord, let this
Christmas be all about preparing for You. Amen.*

DAY 4

Keeping Our Home in Order!

Truly, I say to you, he will dress himself for service and have them recline at table, and he will come and serve them. If he comes in the second watch, or in the third, and finds them awake, blessed are those servants! But know this, that if the master of the house had known at what hour the thief was coming, he would not have left his house to be broken into. You also must be ready, for the Son of Man is coming at an hour you do not expect.

—Luke 12:37–40 (ESV)

Wait for the LORD; be strong, and let your heart take courage; wait for the LORD!

—Psalm 27:14

Remember, yesterday we talked about the fact that we are to "keep our lamps burning" and stand beside the door and wait so that we "may open the door to the Master [Jesus] at once when he comes and knocks." We must be ready to usher Jesus into our own home and have Him look around and find us prepared for his return, our house in order, and our lamps lit.

Jesus was telling His disciples and is telling us today that in order for us to be faithful servants and fulfill the Master's wishes, we must set aside our own personal plans, goals, hopes, and dreams. Why? Because our faithfulness will so fill the Master's heart with joy that He will call us in and have us sit down at the dinner table and dine with Him. Jesus teaches us that true leaders serve. They are out to meet the needs of others. We must know that the Creator of the universe continues to wash the feet of His faithful servants throughout the ages. "The least shall be greatest!" We will be prepared this Christmas season when we become the most humble of servants.

Jesus told His disciples to be careful, for we don't know when the Lord is coming. Jesus says be ready on the second watch (between 9:00 pm and midnight) and on the third watch (midnight to 3:00 am). In fact, He calls us to be ready on every watch. Have you ever noticed that it is easier to be ready on the first watch than the second or third? It really doesn't matter when He returns; if we are to be found faithful, then we must know and expect His presence every second of the day. Since Jesus said, "I'm coming again," then we know

He is, and we should live like it by being prepared. We must be ready, but might we be reminded that being ready does not include looking down at our watches. It does not include arranging our lives as if He's not coming today, so I will prepare some other day.

God is calling us to make sure our homes are prepared for His return. In other words, we must prepare and protect our homes. How? Colossians 3:12–13NKJV says, "As the elect of God holy and beloved, put on tender mercies, kindness, humility, meekness, longsuffering; bearing with one another, and forgiving one another." In our homes, we need to be prepared by living out the Fruit of the Spirit. Our homes should be models to others. Not perfect and without issue, but working on forgiveness and "admonishing each other in psalms and hymns and spiritual songs, singing with grace in your hearts to the Lord." By doing this, we protect our home from the enemy who is looking for any opportunity to break our homes apart. We prepare for the King by keeping our homes at peace as much as possible.

Lord, help us to be prepared by being faithful to You every second of the day. Lord, and as the psalmist cried out to You, may we cry out, "I wait for the LORD, my soul waits, and in Your word I hope; my soul waits for the Lord, more than those who watch for the morning" (Ps. 130:5–6). Amen.

Fully Prepared

I kept looking in the night visions, and behold, with the
clouds of heaven one like a Son of Man was coming, and
He came up to the Ancient of Days and was presented
before Him. And to Him was given dominion, glory
and a kingdom, that all the peoples, nations, and men
of every language might serve Him. His dominion is
an everlasting dominion which will not pass away; and
His kingdom is one which will not be destroyed.

—Daniel 7:13–14

A few days ago, we began looking at our Christmas in the light
of Advent. So far, we have talked about being prepared for the
coming of Christ because that is what Christmas is about, and
being prepared is the specific focus for the first week of Advent.
Advent seeks to remind us to be ready for Jesus's return for

us. Preparing for Jesus's arrival is exactly what the Christmas season is all about or should be about for the child of God, isn't it? The first Christmas, God called His people to be prepared for the coming of the Messiah, and now the Messiah has called us to be prepared for His return. This realization for many of us makes us take a hard look at what our Christmases have become, doesn't it?

This time, instead of being announced by an angel and directed by a star, we will be shaken by the sound of a trumpet's call as Jesus comes like a thief in the night. There will be no need to be directed by a star because when we are His, then the very Spirit of God, the same Spirit that rose Jesus from the grave, lives in us and will guide us. As contrary to the nature as it is for a thief to announce when he was going to break in and steal all that is of value in that home, so it is contrary to the behavior of the Master (Jesus) to announce when he's going to return. After all, it is His house anyway, and He is free to show up anytime he wants, isn't He? That is why we must always be prepared. Jesus's return is imminent and at any moment. The problem for most of us is that if He came right now, we would not be prepared because our house is not in order. Listen, Jesus doesn't have to give anybody a warning, and He won't. He's in charge, and He has a plan that involves you and me as His church and His people being faithful servants.

In the Scripture, we discover that Jesus our Lord and Risen Savior will come again in three stages. The first stage is called the "Rapture." This is the day that our faith in

Jesus Christ has prepared us for. In the second stage Jesus judges the faithfulness of the works of every believer. This is often referred to as the "judgment seat [Bema] of Christ" (2 Corinthians 5:10). At this judgment, Christians will receive degrees of reward for their works or service to God. This is what we are preparing for or being sanctified for. The third stage is the Great White Throne of Judgment. This will occur at the end of the millennium (Revelation 20:11–15). This is the judgment for unbelievers in which they are judged according to their works and sentenced to everlasting punishment in the Lake of Fire. This is not what we are preparing for as His children. We who are saved are preparing for stage two. Philippians 1:6–10 (emphasis added) says,

> And I am sure of this, that he who began a good work in you will bring it to completion at the day of Jesus Christ. It is right for me to feel this way about you all, because I hold you in my heart, for you are all partakers with me of grace, both in my imprisonment and in the defense and confirmation of the gospel. For God is my witness, how I yearn for you all with the affection of Christ Jesus. And it is my prayer that your love may abound more and more, with knowledge and all discernment, so that you may approve what is excellent, and so be pure and blameless for the *day of Christ*."

At Christ's first coming, He is coming as a "thief in the night" and "at an hour that we do not know." During this stage, our Lord will return to this earth only for His children. According to God's Word, we know that this coming will be sometime before or in the middle of the great tribulation mentioned in Daniel and in Revelation. Those who have truly placed their faith in Jesus have given Him their whole heart and lives and won't have to worry about when He comes because they will have no trouble recognizing Him because they were faithful, sanctified, and well prepared for the day of Christ. But for those who haven't surrendered and trusted all to Jesus (as good a people as they may be, no matter how religious they were or how may years they have attended church), they will not see him. They won't recognize Him because they weren't prepared. Jesus is the only way, and to be His, we must choose Him. We must learn to love Jesus in such a way that our love for anyone or anything else looks like hate in comparison. We must seek His kingdom and His will and allow Him to add His righteousness to our lives. Jesus is coming! Are you ready?

In the third stage the whole world will see His return. There will be no denying this one as "every knee will bow and every tongue confess that Jesus is Lord." This time, we (the church) will return with Him and so will the angels as Jesus comes to judge the nations and establish His divine rule on earth for a thousand years.

We are prepared by our faith in Christ, and then our faithfulness to Christ prepares us for the day of Christ.

Christmas is all about being prepared for the coming of Christ. Are you prepared?

Lord, help make sure that our homes are in order, our stewardship honoring, and Lord, as your righteousness is added to us, may we "approve what is excellent, and so be pure and blameless for the day of Christ." Amen.

What God Has Prepared for Those Who Love Him

But as it is written, "What no eye has seen, nor ear heard,
nor the heart of man imagined, what God has prepared
for those who love him" these things God has revealed to
us through the Spirit. For the Spirit searches everything,
even the depths of God. For who knows a person's thoughts
except the spirit of that person, which is in him? So also no
one comprehends the thoughts of God except the Spirit
of God. Now we have received not the spirit of the world,
but the Spirit who is from God, that we might understand
the things freely given us by God. And we impart this in
words not taught by human wisdom but taught by the Spirit,
interpreting spiritual truths to those who are spiritual.

—1 Corinthians 2:9–13 (ESV)

I love to think about the amazing things God has prepared for me. Though I love to think and ponder on these things, my human intellect does not give me wisdom enough to comprehend them. In this passage, Paul is quoting from Isaiah 64:4. He tells us that until the day that the Holy Spirit was given, men did not understand the mystery of the Gospel, but now God has revealed this mystery through the His Spirit. Just as Jesus promised (John 16:12–13). The Holy Spirit came to guide those who penned His Word by revealing every word (2 Pet. 1:20–21). The Holy Spirit moved the writer to write exactly what God wanted written down. If God had not done this, there would be no way for us to know and follow His will. God's written word is one of those amazing things God prepared for us. Just like anything God prepares for us, we can't obtain it on our own. The only way for us to receive it and apply it is to have the Holy Spirit residing in us. The Holy Spirit is a gift only for those who have trusted and given their lives to the Son. The Holy Spirit is the gift of both God the Father and God the Son. Jesus promised that after His departure, He and God the Father would send the Holy Spirit to assist the apostles in their mission to spread the message of God. Peter stated in Acts 2:38 that the Spirit would be a gift to all who believe. Paul states emphatically that He received God's word from the Holy Spirit. That is the way we receive it as well. Many will not accept His Word, many will try to interpret His Word by using worldly knowledge, and others will receive it but refuse to live it. This thinking and living is false doctrine because the Bible did not come from men (2 Pet. 1:21). As believers, we can know what God has prepared for us and wants for us by the power of the Holy Spirit. Listen today, as the Spirit searches our lives, He will always reveal only the Truth. The Spirit searches everything! You and I can't hide anything from God because the Spirit will search it out. He knows our thoughts, but more than that, the Holy Spirit knows God's thoughts. We can't rationalize our way through life because God has a specific plan for us. We can't know His plan without the Holy Spirit. We must stop trying to comprehend God's will, ways, and plans for us through human wisdom or logic. When we do, we are only led further away from what God has prepared for us. God has given you and me as believers all that is needed know and to live His plans. God wants those who love Him to know all He has prepared. The Holy Spirit goes one step further as He gives us the wisdom and power to live out this day what God has prepared for us. God has prepared for us three of the greatest Christmas gifts we could ever want. He gives us His Son, His Word and His Spirit. These are gifts that keep on giving.

> *Lord, help us to cherish the gifts that You have prepared for us, and may these gift daily prepare us for eternity, in Jesus's mighty name, Amen.*

DAY 7

Living Like We Are Ready!

Since therefore Christ suffered in the flesh, arm
yourselves with the same way of thinking, for whoever
has suffered in the flesh has ceased from sin, so as
to live for the rest of the time in the flesh no longer
for human passions but for the will of God.

—1 Peter 4:1–2

It is so easy to blend in these days. It is true. We love to get lost in the crowd. In other words, we don't particularly want to stick out or draw attention to ourselves as being different. So we go with the flow. It doesn't matter whether we are at church or hanging out with friends; we don't want to stick out like a sore thumb, so our action resembles their actions. Some may be thinking, I see the problem with looking or acting like unsaved people, but I do see anything wrong with looking or acting like the people I go to church with. Have we forgotten that "we are all sinners and fall short of the glory of God?" So why would we look like another sinner when we have mastered that on our own? We should edify each other, fellowship with one another, and be unified with each other, but never imitate one another. We are to be like Jesus. We are to be imitators of the Savior and not others who also fall short. When we imitate anyone other than Jesus, we are not living as though we are ready for His return. Our daily goal should be to move closer to Him and look more like Him. The very word *Christian* that we use to define those that follow Jesus demands that we be like Him. Since Jesus Christ suffered for us in the flesh, we are to arm ourselves also with the same mind! We must be willing to suffer for Him and for others as we share the good news with them. God calls to commit to being armed with the mind of Christ. In these last days, we need to have a commitment to God that will endure even the greatest temptations and struggles. He who has suffered in the flesh has ceased from sin! When a person has suffered physical persecution for the sake of Jesus Christ, it changes their whole perspective. So we begin to see sin and the pursuit of the lusts of the flesh more clearly, and when we do, we are less likely to live the rest of our time in the flesh, or for the lusts of men but for the will of God. Oh, believer, we have spent enough time living like the world. Especially, since we are called to live like Jesus. Due to the fact that we are to live like Him, it is a profound, foolish, and a total waste of time for us to live like the world. So we must cease living as though we are double-minded and start living as though we are Christ-minded. The sad truth is that so many people who call themselves Christians are unwilling to commit to Jesus this way because they think that they need to experience more of the world or enjoy a few more fleshly desires before they are willing to fully commit to God. This is tragic, and it leads us in the opposite direction and away from the eternal life we are to live. We must make sure that we are prepared for the day of Christ this Christmas season as we store up our treasures in heaven instead filling and fueling the flesh. It is time that we fully commit to Jesus and start living like we are ready! Take the opportunity to start right now! Jesus will not delay His return just because you aren't ready!

> *Lord, help us to begin living as though we are ready this Christmas and may we do so until You return for us, In Jesus's name.*

All Hope Is in the Savior!

For God alone, O my soul, wait in silence,
for my hope is from him.

—Psalm 62:5

DAY 8

Our Hope Is Absolute!

And now, O Lord, for what do I wait? My hope is in you.

—Psalm 39:7 (ESV)

Here we are facing the second week of Advent. If you remember, the first week of Advent was to help us understand that we are to be prepared for the coming of Christ as the word *advent* originates from the Latin word *advenio* which means "coming to." Every day of Advent and the entire Christmas season is about focusing on Jesus's coming. This second week of the Christmas season teaches us that not only are we to be prepared for Jesus' return, but all our hope is in the return of Christ. Therefore, second week of Advent and the second week of the Christmas season are to help us remember the hope we have in Jesus Christ.

Jeremiah 29:11 tells us that it has always been part of God's plan to give us a future and a hope. A future and a hope is exactly what we find in Jesus. The word *hope* has two meanings in the Bible. The first, *tiqvah* means eager anticipation or waiting, and the second, *elpis* is expectation based on certainty or confidently waiting. The hope we have in Jesus is a hope that leads us to wait confidently for the Lord because God is faithful to His promises. We know that God will do what He says He will do. He will do so in His infinite power, wisdom, and His timing will be perfect.

Where is your hope this Christmas season? Is it in you finances, your family, your job, or the anticipation of the newest and best gifts? Or is it in Jesus alone? All our hope should be wrapped up in Jesus. He is our future and our hope. He is what God promised and continues to promise. Jesus is and always will be God's plan for humanity. Plans that began to unfold at creation. Plans that have continued to unfold throughout history. Plans that only God could cause to come about. Plans that began fully operational in the little town of Bethlehem that Christmas morn with the birth of the long-hoped-for Messiah and that continue to be fully operational today, this Christmas season, as we confidently hope for Jesus' triumphant return.

This week of Advent reminds us that our hope should be totally wrapped up in Jesus! He is our hope.

Lord, help us to remember always the hope we have in You. Help us to never attempt to replace the hope we have in You alone with anything else even if it looks like hope. Lord, help us this Christmas season to unwrap Your gift of hope every day.
Amen.

DAY 9

All I Want for Christmas

He who supplies seed to the sower and bread for food will supply and multiply your seed for sowing and increase the harvest of your righteousness. You will be enriched in every way to be generous in every way, which through us will produce thanksgiving to God. For the ministry of this service is not only supplying the needs of the saints but is also overflowing in many thanksgivings to God. By their approval of this service, they will glorify God because of your submission that comes from your confession of the gospel of Christ, and the generosity of your contribution for them and for all others, while they long for you and pray for you, because of the surpassing grace of God upon you. Thanks be to God for his inexpressible gift!

—2 Corinthians 9:10–15 (esv)

Thanks be to God for His indescribable gift (2 Cor. 9:15)! Have you ever been hesitant to accept a gift? Maybe you just felt so undeserving and so unworthy that you just could not accept what was being offered. The gift was so valuable, and the price that was paid was so much that you just couldn't accept such a gift. We must remember that a gift is not a gift unless it is accepted. God gave us the greatest Christmas gift ever. I know that the price of this gift is way too high. Not to mention the ultimate price the Gift would pay because He loves us that much. God loves us so much that He gave His Son. Listen really clearly, there is something you must know about any gift, especially this one. Ownership is conditional to acceptance. It is not that we ever own the gift that God gives, but instead the Gift owns us. Like any gift, we won't be forced to accept it, or it is no longer a gift. God would never force His gift on us. He does, however, desire with all His heart that we accept it! We need to trust God when He tells us that we will never qualify for such an amazing gift. We can we ever be good enough, or have enough to qualify, but nevertheless, God diligently wants us to accept His life-changing gift this season. All we have to do is trust Him and receive the gift of His Son, Jesus Christ, by faith. This gift is a gift that has eternal consequences for those that accept it or reject it. For those that refuse His gift, they will find themselves eternally hopeless, eternally lost, and will spend the rest of their lives completely isolated from God. Why? Because they have intentionally rejected God's offer of love, grace, mercy, and forgiveness. When we accept His gift, we immediately have an eternal supply of grace, comfort, peace, forgiveness, mercy, and His unconditional love. The greatest sin that we could ever commit is to refuse God's gift. To refuse His gift is to refuse His love. Please don't make that mistake. If you have already accepted His gift, Jesus should be the number one gift that you give this Christmas. Will He be? Jesus is the gift that gives for an eternity. You see, when you have hope you are to give hope.

Lord, help us to recognize that all our hope is wrapped up in the most incredible gift ever given, Jesus.
Amen.

DAY 10

Our Hope Is Complete!

Therefore, preparing your minds for action, and being
sober-minded, set your hope fully on the grace that will
be brought to you at the revelation of Jesus Christ.

—1 Peter1:13

As we press on during this second week of this Christmas
season or Advent we continue to prepare for Christ, and we
set our hearts and our minds on the hope that we have in
Him. Remember as we said yesterday, the hope that we have
is not wishful thinking. It's not the attitude, "I don't know if
it's going to happen, but I hope it happens." The hope we have
in Christ is absolute and eternal because it is in Him and Him
alone. He is worth more than all the wealth in the world. He
is absolutely righteous and holy, and He is perfectly faithful.

The hope that we set our hearts and minds on as Christians is a complete hope in Jesus. It is a confidence that what He promises He will do, what He starts He completes, and who He is will never change. We can always on God.

We know that our hope is in Jesus, but how does our hope grow so large that there is no longer room for doubt, worry, fear, and anxiety? Have you ever noticed that the Christmas season has the tendency to become very stressful for many people? It is true. Instead of being "most wonderful time of the year" Christmas has become the "most stressful time of the year." Why? I believe it is because the expectation or the bar has been set so high that the fear of failure or disappointment begins to flood the hearts and minds of too many during this time of year. They want to get people what they want, and fear the disappointment of others if they can't live up to those expectations. Oh, how we have made Christmas something that God never intended it to be. All because we have placed our hope in other things and other people. Christ alone is our future and our hope. Therefore, our hope can be comingled with other things or other people. It must remain in Christ alone.

We are so tempted to buy into the name it and claim it lie that so many are teaching today. Many tell us that if we give God our health, time, money, and talent, then God will bless us right back in those exact same ways, but we forget what it is that the promises of God truly are when we think that they are physical and monetary. Can they be? Absolutely, but God blesses us so that He might be glorified by what He provided in the first place.

God knows there are earthly blessings we need and want, but God is the dispenser of those according to His will. Make no mistake, those things are not His treasures. He wants us to be much more wealthy than that. True wealth is spiritual wealth, and God's blessings are spiritual blessings. He has blessed us with every *spiritual blessing* in Christ (Eph. 1:3). There are things better and higher than material blessings, and God wants us to have His best. He wants us to have things that last—things that moth and rust won't destroy. We were never intended to put our hope in monetary blessings, but instead, in spiritual blessings. Blessings like the satisfaction of knowing that our sins are forgiven eternally, and the blessing of an eternal inheritance, which is the blessing of a quality of life that is grounded in eternal fellowship with God. In Christ, God offers to give us spiritual blessings and crown us with glory and honor.

The hope that we have is that God delivers perfectly and fully everything we need for our spiritual well-being. God does what He says and delivers what He promises, establishing His sufficiency and power to supply everything we need so that we might bring Him glory. This life is not about God giving us a few things to get us by or get us started. It is not God simply pointing us in the right direction. It is not a matter of God giving us a few pieces of the puzzle and leaving us to figure the rest out. No, this life is about God providing it all.

"Blessed be the God and Father of our Lord Jesus Christ, who has blessed us with every spiritual blessing" (Eph. 1:3). The hope that we have is that Christ alone provides everything we need for salvation, for spiritual nourishment, for instruction, for life, and preparation for His arrival and eternity with Him. Yes, our confidence this Christmas and from this point on is that God supplies it all in Christ—every provision, every instruction, every motivation, every reason, every promise, and every spiritual blessing.

Lord, prepare our minds for action and help us be sober-minded, setting our hope fully on the grace that was brought to us at the revelation of Jesus. Lord, help us to set our minds and hearts on the treasures of heaven so that what we store up will have eternal value for Your glory alone. Amen.

DAY 11

Our Hope Is Built on Nothing Less!

Blessed is he whose help is the God of Jacob,
whose hope is in the LORD his God, the Maker
of heaven and earth, the sea, and everything in
them—the LORD, who remains faithful forever.

—Psalms 146:5–6)

On this second week of Advent and the Christmas season we prepare for the coming of Christ, and we are led to hope. On our journey this week, we have found that Christian hope is certain anticipation. On this journey of hope, one will find that love, faith, and hope go hand in hand. They have three separate meanings, but they are meaningless without the other. First Corinthians 13:13 (NLT) says, "Three things will last forever—faith, hope, and love—and the greatest of these is love."

Today, let's simply talk about how the hope we have only in Christ is built upon. To do so, we must talk about those three inseparable treasures mentioned—faith, hope, and love. Jesus is the total package of love and hope. He is love and He is our only hope. Love is an action and a sacrifice. For example, Jesus said, "No greater love has any man than to lay down his life for his friend or brother" (John 15:13). Jesus demonstrated love perfectly. Therefore, He is the perfect example of love because He is love. The love of Christ leads us to hope in Christ, and hope in Christ always leads us back to the love of Christ. They are eternal and a complete circle. They never end and they keep running into one another.

What about faith? The writer of Hebrew tells us that "faith is the assurance of things hoped for" (Heb. 11:1). Faith cannot be moved by circumstances nor what the eyes see because though God is unseen, He is seen clearly in His faithfulness. Just as hope is dependent upon love and love leads us to hope, hope results in faith, and faith also brings hope with it. Faith is where our hope is being built upon. Therefore, faith and hope are connected as well. Together, faith, hope, and love ensure that our lives are built upon an unshakable confidence in God.

Faith is given by God to know God. The more we know Him, the more we love Him, and the more we love Him, the more our hope is built up in Him, and the more our hope is built up in Him, the greater our faith becomes. The object of faith and hope is God alone.

Hope is faith's anchor in who God is. This is vital. When we understand God rightly, then our hope says, "All things are possible with God." On the other hand, when we misunderstand who God is, our faith wanes because we have no hope.

The proof of our faith is and always will be hope. When we have hope in God then we prove it by a that is active and true.

But without love and faith, hope is only a powerless wish. But when we love God and our hope is wrapped up in God, our faith becomes powerful confidence. When our hope is but a wish, it's something we long for, but it's generally not connected to God. Biblical hope has a firm foundation only in Jesus Christ.

My hope is built on nothing less than Jesus's blood and righteousness. I dare not trust the sweetest frame but wholly lean on Jesus's name. On Christ, the solid Rock, I stand. All other ground is sinking sand.

What is your hope built upon this Christmas season?

Lord, may our hope be built up in You alone
this Christmas season. Amen.

DAY 12

Our Hope Never Runs Dry!

> May the God of hope fill you with all joy and
> peace in believing, so that by the power of the
> Holy Spirit you may abound in hope.
>
> —Romans 15:13

On our Christmas journey through hope this week, we have found that the hope we have in Jesus is a hope that leads us to wait confidently for the Lord because He is faithful to His promises. "For in this hope we were saved. Now hope that is seen is not hope. For who hopes for what he sees? But if we hope for what we do not see, we wait for it with patience" (Rom. 8:24–25**)**.

We have found that the hope we have in Christ is absolute and eternal because it is based on who He is and what He can do. Jesus is worth more than all the wealth in the world. He is absolutely righteous and holy, and He is perfectly faithful. The hope that we set our hearts and minds on this Christians is a complete hope in Jesus. Therefore, Jesus and His kingdom are the treasures that we seek. The treasure that God wants to give us is the priceless treasure of making us more like His Son.

Hope is an essential spiritual and emotional component of life. Without it, we live in despair. Hope endures. The nature of the hope we have is a foundationally spiritual hope. The good life as some would call it, the life of peace and prosperity, is not guaranteed by God, but true hope, the hope that we find in Jesus, endures all things. So many of the heroes of the faith both past and present testify to this (Heb. 11).

The hope that endures is the assurance that "God works out all things for the good of those who love Christ Jesus, and who have been called according to His purposes" (Rom. 8:28).

We have talked about the fact that we have a hope to build upon. We have a hope in Jesus that is eternal. We have a hope that is built on nothing less that Jesus' blood and righteousness, and He is the foundation of hope, and the Holy Spirit with faith and love is building upon the hope that we have in Jesus.

> Through him we have also obtained access by faith into this grace in which we stand, and we rejoice in hope of the glory of God. More than that, we rejoice

in our sufferings, knowing that suffering produces endurance, and endurance produces character, and character produces hope, and hope does not put us to shame, because God's love has been poured into our hearts through the Holy Spirit who has been given to us. (Rom. 5:2–5)

There is so much more that could be said about the perfect hope that we find in Jesus. God's Word has much to say about that hope. We must realize that "whatever was written in former days was written for our instruction, that through endurance and through the encouragement of the Scriptures we might have hope" (Rom. 15:4). God is giving us and building in us a hope that endures all things. Do you have a hope that endures all things and never runs dry? That is the hope that we must share this Christmas.

Lord, God of hope, may You fill us completely with all joy and peace in believing so that by the power of the Holy Spirit, we may abound in hope. Amen.

DAY 13

Jesus Is Our Hope!

To them God chose to make known how great
among the Gentiles are the riches of the glory of this
mystery, which is Christ in you, the hope of glory.

—Colossians 1:27 (ESV)

As we close in on the end of our second week of the Christmas season, the week of hope, we can't help but ask our self, "Where is my hope?" Especially in light of the fact that we have discovered that true hope has one source, and that source is Jesus. We now know that once we discover and surrender to the Source of all hope, then our hope will never end, and this eternal hope is the only foundation worth building upon.

Our hope, blessings, and purposes are summed up "in Christ." The purpose of history is to bring all things under the headship of Jesus Christ, and as they do, their purpose is wrapped up in glorifying the Father.

Our hope includes the work of the Father, Son, and Holy Spirit, and it considers eternity past, present, and future. Therefore, our future and our hope are not limited to mere treasures on this earth. No, our hope is wrapped up, storing the treasures of heaven, seeking first the kingdom of God, and glorifying God alone in thought and action.

Our inheritance is hope fulfilled, but it is also a future blessing. It is one which will be fully realized after the second coming of Christ. That is what we are preparing for this Christmas season and this second week of Advent. As mentioned, our blessings are "in the heavenly places in Christ" (Eph. 1:3), the culmination of which comes at the second coming of Christ, when all things are "summed up in Him" (Eph. 1:10). God's purpose is that we will someday stand "holy and blameless before Him" (Eph. 1:4). That is why we are being sanctified or prepared now! There is no time for waiting. We can't say with our hearts and minds, "There is plenty of time to prepare. I will do it later." Jesus is coming like a thief in the night. I pray that it is today, but many can't pray that because though they know Christ as Savior, and they refuse to surrender to Him as Lord. The time to prepare is right now and every day until Christ returns.

Listen, our hope is built up by what is laid up in heaven and not by any treasure that we have laid up for ourselves on this dying and decaying earth. In Colossians 1, Paul says,

"We always thank God, the Father of our Lord Jesus Christ, when we pray for you, since we heard of your faith in Christ Jesus and of the love that you have for all the saints (Col. 1:3–4, ESV). Remember, our faith, love in Christ, and our hope, are all stored up in heaven. How do they get stored up? "Because of the hope laid up for you in heaven, of which you previously heard in the word of truth, the gospel" (Col. 1:5). As we hear the word of truth or the Gospel, we are moved to put feet to our faith, and as we do, the love that we sow results in treasure being laid up in heaven. Heaven is the only sure thing worth investing in, and Jesus is the only access point.

> In him we have obtained an inheritance, having been predestined according to the purpose of him who works all things according to the counsel of his will, so that we who were the first to hope in Christ might be to the praise of his glory. In him you also, when you heard the word of truth, the gospel of your salvation, and believed in him, were sealed with the promised Holy Spirit, who is the guarantee of our inheritance until we acquire possession of it, to the praise of his glory. (Eph. 1:11–14, ESV)

Lord, I thank you that You alone God chose to make known the riches of Your glory to us. I praise You that this is no longer a mystery once we realize that Christ in us is our only hope of glory. Father, I thank you for the hope for us is a surety in Your Son, and, Holy Spirit, help us to clearly reflect the image that You gave new life in us this Christmas season and until the Son returns.

Amen.

What Christmas Brings

And the angel said to them, "Fear not, for behold, I bring you good news of great joy that will be for all the people.

—Luke 2:10 (ESV)

Christmas seems to come quicker and quicker every year. After kicking off the New Year, it seems like no time and its Christmas again. Well, it is that time again. Christmas Day is quickly approaching, and everywhere we look, we see the joys of Christmas all around. Whoa…hold on just a minute. Joys are all around! It seems like chaos for many of us, right? What do you mean joy? Have you seen how expensive gifts will be? Christmas brings a variety of responses. What does Christmas bring for you? Does it bring gifts under the tree, lights all around, cards in the mail, chestnuts on an open fire, dinners with family and friends, stockings hanging on the fireplace, the sweet sounds of Christmas carols, and cries of Merry Christmas ringing for the street? For many, Christmas is fun and merry, but for others, it is stressful and a time of sorrow. For many, there is not enough money to buy the loved ones what they want for Christmas. Others are saddened as they think of loved ones who will not be able to come home for Christmas, and there are even others, who have grown so acclimatized to receiving that the thought of giving is a burden. What does Christmas really bring? As the angel declared, "I bring you good news of great joy that will be for all people." Christmas is meant to be a time of great joy. It is a time that reminds us of God's great love for us. It is meant to be a time of sharing, healing, and renewal. You see, the angel was declaring the birth of the Savior. He is the reason we celebrate. It is His love that should flood our souls this and every Christmas season. Jesus's birth brought good news that is to be great joy as it is shared with the world. Think about the excitement the angel was sharing! This was no ordinary baby. The prophets had told of His coming decades before. What does your heart say Christmas brings? Where is your excitement to share "good news of great joy"? Simeon, when He saw the child Jesus said, "Behold this child is set for the fall and rising of many in Israel and for a sign that is spoken against…that the thoughts of many hearts may be revealed" (Luke 2:34–35). Christmas is to be a time of sharing the good news because the good news brings us great joy! Allow

Jesus to rule your heart, your soul, and your mind, and let Him fill you with joy this Christmas. The best way to sustain and grow in joy is to give the joy of His love away! Give it this Christmas like never before. So what does Christmas bring? It brings love, joy, peace, patience, kindness, goodness, faithfulness, gentleness, self-control, and "good news of great joy." And all this was delivered as the Savior was born Christmas morn.

Lord, help us to recognize the joy that Christmas brings,
Amen.

WEEK 3

Consumed with Joy!

My soul longs, yes, faints for the courts of the LORD;
my heart and flesh sing for joy to the living God.

—Psalm 84:2

DAY 15

Filled with joy

So do not let what you regard as good be spoken of as evil. For the kingdom of God is not a matter of eating and drinking but of righteousness and peace and joy in the Holy Spirit. Whoever thus serves Christ is acceptable to God and approved by men. So then let us pursue what makes for peace and for mutual upbuilding.

—Romans 14:16–19 (ESV)

Here, we are already to the third week of the Christmas season. So far, we have been preparing for Jesus's return, and we have been seeking and building upon true hope. This third week of Advent or the Christmas season, we are reminded to be filled with joy. "May the God of hope fill you with all joy and peace in believing, so that by the power of the Holy Spirit you may abound in hope" (Rom. 15:13, ESV).

It is amazing how every eternal quality that God provides is interrelated and dependent upon the other. Love, joy, peace, faith, hope, etc., are all never-ending qualities that cause each other to abound. Similar, to how true hope requires love, joy, and faith, the same can be said of any fruit of the Spirit or characteristic of Jesus. Jesus was and is the perfect representation of perfection and each and every fruit. Therefore, His Spirit is the true source for any and all of them.

But today, we are talking about being filled with joy. Notice in Romans 15 that God is the source of "all joy." That means that there is no joy without God. Why? Because there is no hope, no love, no peace, and no believing or faith with out God. Proverbs 10:28 says that the hope of righteousness brings joy, and 1 Peter 1:8 says, "Though you have not seen him, you love him. Though you do not now see him, you believe in him and rejoice with joy that is inexpressible and filled with glory…" And Romans 14:17 says, "For the kingdom of God is not a matter of eating and drinking but of righteousness and peace and joy in the Holy Spirit." This life is a matter of seeking after righteousness (Jesus), and as we seek after Jesus, we are filled with joy.

How do we seek Jesus? Well, we seek Him by seeking His kingdom and His righteousness (Matt. 6:33). How do we make sure that we are seeking His kingdom and righteousness? We find in Luke 2:9–10 (emphasis added) that when the "angel of the Lord appeared to them, and the glory of the Lord shone around them, and they were filled with great fear. And the angel said to them, 'Fear not, for behold, I bring you *good news of great joy* that will be for all the people.'" The Gospel of Jesus Christ is good news. It is eternal and remains forever. It is the best news imaginable for absolutely everybody and everything. It is not merely good news for the few, but for all! Jesus is the atoning sacrifice not merely for the sins of Christians but for the sins of the whole world (1 John 2:2). The Creator is the Redeemer of His creation (Col. 1:15–20). Whether people know that truth or not does not make or determine its truth. It depends entirely on Jesus. It is not dependent on any human action or human response of any kind. Jesus said, "For God so loved the world that he gave His only Son, so that everyone who believes in Him will not not perish but may have eternal life" (John 3:16). The good news is that when we trust God's grace to save us through the work of Jesus, our sins are forgiven, we get a purpose for living, we're promised a future home in heaven, and we are filled with joy.

As Rick Warren said, "God has never made a person He didn't love. Everybody matters to Him. When Jesus stretched out his arms wide on the cross, He was saying, 'I love you this much!'" Now that is good news! It is good news that Jesus loves us too much to let our sins destroy us eternally. It is good news that Jesus paid the wages of our sins on the cross and He rose from the dead, defeating the grave, so that we can spend an eternity with Him. It is good news that Jesus went to be with the Father, but is returning for His own.

The good news is good news for everyone even if you have never trusted Jesus as Lord and Savior. The good news is that there is still time and that Jesus paid the price for you. All that you have to do is believe in your heart and confess with your mouth that Jesus is Lord and Savior and you are saved. It is not the words that save you, but the Savior who saves you. He is always faithful to do as He promised, and that is good news. When our eyes and hearts are upon the good news of Jesus Christ this Christmas season, we will be filled with great joy.

Lord, thank you for the good news! Thank you for loving me and saving me, and, Lord, help me wait well for Your return and may Your joy be complete in me. Amen.

A Christmas-Minded Life

Those who live according to the sinful nature have their
minds set on what that nature desires; but those who live
in accordance with the Spirit have their minds set on
what the Spirit desires. The mind of sinful man is death,
but the mind controlled by the Spirit is life and peace

—Romans 8:5–6

Have you ever noticed that whatever we set our minds on
seems to dictate our attitudes, our actions, and our day? Sure,
we tend to blame the shiftiness of our thoughts on a variety
of causes, but God's Word makes it clear that what we set
our minds on is our personal responsibility. My dad used to
tell me, "Son, don't let anyone have the benefit of messing
with your mind," but we do. We blame our mind-set on our

own flesh, other people, our circumstances, the world, and we even give the devil credit at times. We treat our thoughts as though they were this unstoppable freight train destined to crash. We see them as something that we can't control, and that is so untrue according to God's Word. It is true, however, that we have so many unwelcoming thoughts, but they are not unstoppable. God gave us verses like our verses today to remind us of the simple truth that "the mind is controlled by the Spirit in this life." So we do have a choice in what we think about. We have a choice whether to "set your minds on things above, not on earthly things" (Col. 3:2). Mark Twain said, "Drag your thoughts away from your troubles…by the ears, by the heels, or any other means." What we think about is always a choice we make. We must stop letting our excuses for our wrong thinking deem them unstoppable. The reason our thoughts become unstoppable is because we set our mind on that falsehood. It is true; so many of us have a tendency toward wrong thinking and worry, but it is only because we think on things and dwell on certain situations instead focusing on the answer to life, Jesus. We must consistently "cast all our care upon Him, for He cares for us" (1 Pet. 5:7). We have to turn off our own fleshly thoughts and concerns and focus on His eternal blessings. "Count your blessings, name them one by one, count your blessings, see what God has done" (Oatman, 1997). We are to set our minds on the things above and our hearts will follow. For the believer, Christmas simply means Christ more or more of Christ. Therefore, we are to set out minds on Christmas all year round. Every single day we are set our minds on Christ more. When we do, we will see that our troubles aren't so weighty, our trials don't have the sting they once did, and the blessings He gives are so enormous that they drown out any sorrow. Jesus said,

> If you love me, keep my commands. And I will ask the Father, and he will give you another advocate to help you and be with you forever the Spirit of truth. The world cannot accept him, because it neither sees him nor knows him. But you know him, for he lives with you and will be in you. (John 14:15–17)

When we set our minds on Christmas (Christ more), then our life follows suit, and the Spirit takes over, giving us a consistent "life and peace" that can only be found in Jesus. Will you begin today with Christmas-minded thoughts?

Lord, help us to set our minds on things above,
not on earthly things.
Amen.

DAY 17

The Heart of Christmas

For our heart is glad in him, because
we trust in his holy name.

—Psalm 33:21 (ESV)

This third week of advent or the Christmas season is all about joy. The dictionary meaning of *joy* is "the emotion of great delight or happiness caused by something exceptionally good or satisfying." Joy is not happiness. Happiness is temporal, where joy is eternal. Happiness can be found in many sources, like eating chocolate, but joy only has one source—God.

Biblical *joy* comes from the Greek root word *chara*, which means "to be exceedingly glad." In other words, joy is something that goes beyond happiness. James 1:2 says, "Consider it all joy, my brothers, when you encounter various trials." How could we ever consider going through difficulties and trials all joy? We find the answer in James 1:3–4: "Knowing that the testing of our faith produces endurance. And let endurance have its perfect result, that you may be perfect and complete, lacking in nothing." Joy comes as we persevere through various trials because God is there with us to help us, grow our faith, and strengthen our walk.

Happiness depends upon temporal factors, like circumstances or other people, while joy is true contentment that springs forth from our faith in the Lord and is not dependent upon external factors.

Joy is found over 214 times in God's Word, and almost one fourth of those verses are found in the Psalms. Therefore, the best place to get a true sense of joy in our lives is right in the middle of Psalms. There is no doubt that David had his ups and downs and found himself frequently in the middle of uncertain circumstances and persecution, but the joy he found in the Lord was always evident in his life.

Though happiness is an emotion that is often faked, joy on the other hand is not an emotion that cannot be forced, fabricated, or faked. There are times in our lives when joy seems to elude us. This is normal. There will be times in our lives when we will not feel joyful, and yet joy is right there and always present. Though joy is always present, it cannot be forced, but it is meant to fill us at all times.

Joy is not dependent upon our circumstance.

For in the day of trouble He will keep me safe in His dwelling; He will hide me in the shelter of his sacred tent and set me high upon a rock. Then my head will be exalted above the enemies who surround me; at His sacred tent I will sacrifice with shouts of joy; I will sing and make music to the Lord. Hear my voice when I call, Lord; be merciful to me and answer me. (Ps. 27:5–7, NIV)

Even when we find ourselves in the midst of a difficult situation, we should be filled with and experience joy, but we can't fabricate it or fake it. We must simply take hold of it and be filled with it. Jesus said, "Blessed are you when people hate you, when they exclude you and insult you and reject your name as evil, because of the Son of Man. Rejoice in that day and leap for joy, because great is your reward in heaven. For that is how their ancestors treated the prophets" (Luke 6:22–23, NIV). Though our eyes may tell us we are in trouble, our hearts tell us we are safe in the arms of Jesus, and that is where we find joy. Joy is found when we are secure in the Lord.

Joy can always be experienced in difficult situations. How? I believe that we begin to dwell in joy as we understand what it is built upon. I came upon this acronym a while back that helps me understand how joy flourishes despite our circumstances—*J*esus, *O*thers, and *Y*ou. We find joy as we love the Lord our God with all our heart, soul, strength, and mind and love our neighbor as our self. No matter the circumstance or situation when this is the formulated in our lives, then the result will always be joy.

Paul wrote, "Be full of joy in the Lord always. I will say again, be full of joy. Let everyone see that you are gentle and kind. The Lord is coming soon" (Phil. 4:4–5).

Lord, may Your joy in us be complete this Christmas
as we love You the way that we should so that we can
love others no matter the situation or circumstance.
Amen.

DAY 18

A Joyful Purpose

The kingdom of heaven is like treasure hidden in a field.
When a man found it, he hid it again, and then in his
joy went and sold all he had and bought that field.

—Matthew 13:44 (NIV)

On this third week of the Christmas season, we have set out on a journey to know and live in the "great joy" that the good news of Jesus brings. So far, we have discovered many things about joy. We have found that joy is not a temporal feeling or emotion. We have found that joy is not dependent on any situation or circumstance, and it can't be found in other people. We have discovered that God is our eternal source of joy. We found that joy is not happiness, so it cannot be faked, forced, or fabricated. No, joy is manifested and secured the more intimate our relationship with Jesus becomes.

Today, we find that joy comes when we have purpose in our life.

The psalmist said, "You make known to me the path of life; you will fill me with joy in your presence, with eternal pleasures at your right hand" (Ps. 16:11, NIV). Jesus said it this way: "The kingdom of heaven is like treasure hidden in a field. When a man found it, he hid it again, and then in his joy went and sold all he had and bought that field" (Matt. 13:44, NIV). Joy comes from the treasure we seek. Where is your hidden treasure? What is the path of life that God has for you? Are you seeking the fields for the treasure that God has for you?

Joy comes when we live in the eternal presence of God. David said, "Through the victories you gave, his glory is great; you have bestowed on him splendor and majesty. Surely you have granted him unending blessings and made him glad with the joy of your presence. For the king trusts in the Lord; through the unfailing love of the Most High he will not be shaken" (Ps. 21:5–7, NIV). In a world where fame, fortune, success, and money are glorified, it is easy to lose focus and settle for temporal happiness instead of eternal joy. It is easy to invest in the temporal treasures of financial security and moving up the corporate ladder instead of investing in eternal treasures by "seeking first the kingdom of God and His righteousness." This verse says that victories are good, glory is great, and splendor and majesty are their results, but *joy* comes only from investing our time in God's presence.

Joy not only comes from investing our time in the presence of God, but joy comes in investing our life in praising God. The principle of a life of praise should be easier for us to fathom because our local church worship is to be filled with praise. But so often, we find that even our local church worship doesn't meet God's standard for praise or worship at all and has therefore ceased being a consistent place of joy. We are to make sure that our places of worship are places where the sacrifices of joy are consistent. "And now my head shall be lifted up above my enemies all around me; Therefore I will offer sacrifices of joy in His tabernacle; I will sing, yes, I will sing praises to the Lord" (Ps. 27:6, NKJV).

According to the psalmist, singing, clapping, and shouting are all a vital part of joyful worship. Too often, our places for worship have become too religious for these demonstrations of joy.

Luke 19:36–39 says,

> As He [Jesus] went along, people spread their cloaks on the road. When He came near the place where the road goes down the Mount of Olives, the whole crowd of disciples began joyfully to praise God in loud voices for all the miracles they had seen: "Blessed is the king who comes in the name of the Lord!" "Peace in heaven and glory in the highest!" The people shouted, sang praises, and lifted their hands and voices out of the joy of being in the presence of the Lord.

Joy will be evident in our life as we trust and obey God's every word. Jesus says, "If you keep my commands, you will remain in my love, just as I have kept my Father's commands and remain in his love. I have told you this so that my *joy* may be in you and that your *joy* may be complete. My command is this: Love each other as I have loved you" (John 15:10–12, NIV).

There is no greater place to be in our life than in the center of God's will, and there is no way to be in the center of God's will without living according to the Word of God. Where are you this Christmas season? Filled with joy at the center of God's will or seeking your own will and attempting to manufacture happiness?

Lord, help us to move closer to You with every moment, to invest our time in Your presence, and help us to truly praise You by "offering sacrifices of joy." And, Lord, may our joy be evident and complete as trusting and obeying Your every word and Your every command become the way of life for us.
Amen.

DAY 19

Joyfully Persuaded

Our mouths are filled with laughter, our tongues with songs of joy. Then it was said among the nations, "The Lord has done great things for them." The Lord has done great things for us, and we are filled with joy.

—Psalm 126:2–3 (NIV)

As week three draws to an end, I pray that we continue in the good news of great joy. I pray that Jesus becomes our continuous pursuit in life because when He does, then our joy will always be complete.

We will find joy as we continually praise God for what He has already done. "For you make me glad by your deeds, Lord; I sing for joy at what your hands have done. How great are your works, Lord, how profound your thoughts!" (Ps. 92:4–5, NIV).

Oh, listen as the psalmist said, when "our mouths are filled with laughter, our tongues with songs of joy. Then it was said among the nations, 'The Lord has done great things for them.' The Lord has done great things for us, and we are filled with joy!" (Ps. 126:2–3, NIV). A child of God should always be filled with joy because the Lord is our constant focus.

Remember what Paul told Timothy: "I know whom I have believed, and am persuaded that he is able to keep that which I have committed unto him against that day" (2 Tim. 1:12, KJV). Are you persuaded that God will take care of you in every circumstance and every situation? When you are, then you will be filled with joy unspeakable.

Joy will be evident in our lives when people see Christ in us. Paul said,

> So the message of the Lord was spreading through the whole country. But the Jewish people stirred up some of the important religious women and the leaders of the city. They started trouble against Paul and Barnabas and forced them out of their area. So Paul and Barnabas shook the dust off their feet and went to Iconium. But the followers were filled with joy and the Holy Spirit. (Acts 13:49–52, NCV)

There are several other instances where Paul encouraged people who were insulted or rejected because of their faith. He always encouraged them to be joyful because they were suffering on behalf of Christ.

When people don't want you around because of your faith, celebrate joyfully. You are being excluded because they see Jesus living in you.

My friends, do not be surprised at the terrible trouble which now comes to test you. Do not think that something strange is happening to you. But be happy that you are sharing in Christ's sufferings so that you will be happy and full of joy when Christ comes again in glory. When people insult you because you follow Christ, you are blessed, because the glorious Spirit, the Spirit of God, is with you (1 Pet. 4:12–14, NCV).

Lord, may we always remain joyfully persuaded by who You are and what You have done, and may we never fall into the trap of being persuaded by anything or anyone else.
Amen.

DAY 20

Inexpressible and Glorious Joy!

Though you have not seen Him, you love Him; and even though you do not see Him now, you believe in Him and are filled with an inexpressible and glorious joy, for you are receiving the goal of your faith, the salvation of your souls.

—1 Peter 1:8–9

Here, we are upon the last day of our weeklong journey through joy. These first three weeks have reminded us so much about who God is, what He does, and what He will do. Based on that knowledge, we are reminded of who we are, what we must do, and how we must live. God placed 1 Peter 1:8–9 upon my heart to study as we close out this week of joy. Remember, our joy doesn't stop because our study ends today. No, joy is eternal, and it is to be built upon every single day.

In our scripture passage today, we see clearly Peter telling every child of God what it looks like to live the life that we are called to live and, as a result, experience the joy that is only found in Christ Jesus. So let's dive in and see what it looks like in our life when we have that inexpressible joy, or better said, when that inexpressible joy has us.

Peter told them, when you are filled with joy, "You are loving Christ; you are believing in Christ; you are rejoicing in Christ with inexpressible and glorified joy; all of that even though you do not now see him." Why was Peter telling them what joy looks like? So that if they ever drifted away from it, they would have a clear picture to show them what's happening so they could "wake up and return to what they've lost" (John Piper).

John Piper equated what Peter is telling us in 1 Peter 1 to a swimmer who is swimming upstream. He says,

> True Christianity is like swimming upstream in a river of godlessness—for us, secular American godlessness. We swim with the stroke of love to Christ, and the stroke of faith in Christ, and the stroke of joy in Christ. And while we swim, we do not get swept away with the godless toward the terrible cataracts of judgment down river. God keeps us, as verse 5 said, through faith. He enables us to keep on swimming against the stream with the strokes of faith, love, and joy so that we don't get carried away in the current of Christlessness. Our swimming coach, the apostle

Peter, is on the shore watching us and following us. When we are swimming well, he calls out to us, "Look here, you're doing well, I'm putting a flag here even with where you are in the river. Now mark this. This is where you are." That's what he's doing in verses 8 and 9. The reason is so that if we stop using the swimming strokes of love for Jesus, and faith in Jesus, and joy in Jesus, and begin to just float downstream in the river of godlessness, we will be able to wake up and look to the shore and notice that the flag is upstream. We will have a fixed point of reference to call us back to what real Christianity is.

We find joy and reflect who we were created to be as true Christians when we are loving, hoping in, and trusting Christ alone. The Christmas season reminds us of the same thing. Our entire walk or life is to be direct by Jesus alone, and when it is, then love, hope, faith, and joy will shine through. Joy will be evident in our life when people see Christ in us.

> *Lord, help us prepare well and be filled with*
> *inexpressible joy as we "are receiving the goal of*
> *our faith, the salvation of our souls!" Amen.*

WEEK 4

It Is All about the Savior!

For it is for this we labor and strive, because we
have fixed our hope on the living God, who is
the Savior of all men, especially of believers.

—1 Timothy 4:10

Giving Christmas Back

As for the one who is weak in faith, welcome him, but not to quarrel over opinions. One person believes he may eat anything, while the weak person eats only vegetables. Let not the one who eats despise the one who abstains, and let not the one who abstains pass judgment on the one who eats, for God has welcomed him. Who are you to pass judgment on the servant of another? It is before his own master that he stands or falls. And he will be upheld, for the Lord is able to make him stand.

One person esteems one day as better than another, while another esteems all days alike. Each one should be fully convinced in his own mind. The one who observes the day, observes it in honor of the Lord. The one who eats, eats in honor of the Lord, since he gives thanks to God, while the one who abstains, abstains in honor of

the Lord and gives thanks to God. For none of us lives
to himself, and none of us dies to himself. For if we live,
we live to the Lord, and if we die, we die to the Lord.
So then, whether we live or whether we die, we are the
Lord's. For to this end Christ died and lived again, that
he might be Lord both of the dead and of the living.
Why do you pass judgment on your brother? Or you,
why do you despise your brother? For we will all stand
before the judgment seat of God; for it is written,
"As I live, says the Lord, every knee shall bow to me,
and every tongue shall confess to God."
So then each of us will give an account of himself to God.

Do Not Cause Another to Stumble

Therefore let us not pass judgment on one another any
longer, but rather decide never to put a stumbling block
or hindrance in the way of a brother. I know and am
persuaded in the Lord Jesus that nothing is unclean in itself,
but it is unclean for anyone who thinks it unclean. For if
your brother is grieved by what you eat, you are no longer
walking in love. By what you eat, do not destroy the one
for whom Christ died. So do not let what you regard as
good be spoken of as evil. For the kingdom of God is not
a matter of eating and drinking but of righteousness and
peace and joy in the Holy Spirit. Whoever thus serves Christ
is acceptable to God and approved by men. So then let us
pursue what makes for peace and for mutual upbuilding.
Do not, for the sake of food, destroy the work of God.
Everything is indeed clean, but it is wrong for anyone to

make another stumble by what he eats. It is good not to eat meat or drink wine or do anything that causes your brother to stumble. The faith that you have, keep between yourself and God. Blessed is the one who has no reason to pass judgment on himself for what he approves. But whoever has doubts is condemned if he eats, because the eating is not from faith.

For whatever does not proceed from faith is sin.

—Romans 14 (ESV)

I have to confess that Christmas, as we know it today, has largely become something to survive, not celebrate. But before you judge me too severely, I would like to suggest that I may be in good company. There is another I believe feels much like I do. That is Jesus. I can't help but wonder if Jesus enjoys the way most people celebrate Christmas today.

Don't you wish there was a simpler way to celebrate Christmas? I think that if we honest with ourselves then most of us would say that we wished there was a way to celebrate Christmas with less financial stress, less time stress, and less emotional stress, but every year, most of us hop right on that conveyor belt that takes us through the same path every year at this time.

We are stuck with the pattern of meeting all expectations of others and ourselves. What would happen if we were to jump off that conveyor belt this year and say, "I'm going to choose another path this year?" Well, we would hurt and disappoint ourselves and those who depend upon the traditions that we have made, wouldn't we? And since it is not very loving to hurt or disappoint family or friends, we won't change anything even if we wanted to. We just can't.

Christmas has become far more about family traditions, about time spent together as a family, and, of course, about giving and receiving gifts than about celebrating Jesus. These are good things, and if this is what Christmas means to us, let's just be honest about it. Let's stop pretending that it is all about Jesus, when it is really mostly about family, traditions, and gifts. Let's be honest about what Christmas is really about for us.

How many have seen Christmas programs before? How many have heard the Christmas story? Well, if the way we celebrate Christmas was a story or a play, who would honestly have the lead role? Who would be the star? Not who is most important in the play, but who has the biggest parts. I asked myself this question this week. Would it be us, our children, our spouse, our mom, our dad, or our sister or brother? Which characters would take center stage?

The next question I asked myself is, what should our Christmas story really be about? This is not a clear-cut matter for us, is it? There are so many Christmas traditions that we would be better off without! The truth of the matter is that Christmas is a time and a place for acting in faith. Romans 14:5–6 says, "One man considers one day more sacred than another; another man considers every day alike. Each one should be fully convinced in his own mind. He who regards one day as special, does so to the Lord."

Let's use this standard for evaluating our own Christmas story. If you know Christians who do not believe in celebrating Christmas, according to this passage, that's okay. And if you regard Christmas as a special day, that's okay too! As long as we do so unto the Lord. Why? It is not the occasion that is sacred, but instead, the One who is to be celebrated that is important. "He who regards one day as special, does so to the Lord." We must each guard our hearts so that we do not view our own way of observing Christmas as a religious requirement that is necessary for pleasing God or even for salvation. We are saved by grace and not by observing special days.

We celebrate special holidays because we love the Lord, and we do so for His glory. In Galatians 4:8–11, Paul says this to the Galatians,

> Formerly, when you did not know God, you were slaves to those who by nature are not gods. But now that you know God—or rather are known by God— how is it that you are turning back to those weak and miserable principles? Do you wish to be enslaved by them all over again? You are observing special days and months and seasons and years! I fear for you, that somehow I have wasted my efforts on you.

We hear militant cries from conservative Christians that we should take back Christmas from those who have long commercialized it and from those who, over the last twenty years, have increasingly called for the secularization of Christmas. Take it back! But it is not ours to take. It doesn't belong to us. It's not our birthday.

Instead of taking back Christmas, we need to give back Christmas…to Jesus. We need to give it back to Jesus and ask Him what He wants it to be. Many of us get so irritated with those people in our family who either don't ask us what we want or, worse, ask and then get us something else we don't want. Let's ask Jesus what He wants on His birthday and then give it to Him. The way He wants it regardless of our different traditions.

What would Jesus want Christmas to be about? What does He want to be the central part of every celebration regardless of the specifics? Here's a hint: it applies to every other day of the year too and not just Christmas. God wants us to celebrate the life of Jesus within us as we walk in obedience to His Word in all we think, say, and do.

Do our hearts and minds belong to Jesus at Christmas? Do our hearts and minds belong to Jesus the other 364 days of the year? Do we celebrate the birth and life of Christ on Christmas day *and* on every other day of the year? It's hard to show your love and appreciation for someone one day a year if you haven't shown it the rest of the year.

As Christians, we are called to make the most of every opportunity to share Christ, to make Him known to everyone around us. Christmas presents us with unique opportunities to share Jesus Christ with others in ways that would be resisted by nonbelievers and seem pushy to them any other time of year. There is no higher priority for Jesus, no greater gift we can give Him on His birthday than to share Him with others—not just with our words but with our lives. Lay down your expectations for Christmas and take up His expectations for Christmas.

When we do this, we will avoid three of the most common sins of Christmas: anxiety, worldliness, and idolatry (Phil. 4:6–7). Do not be anxious about anything (at Christmas), but in everything, by prayer and petition, with thanksgiving, present your requests to God. And the peace of God, which transcends all understanding, will guard your hearts and your minds in Christ Jesus.

James 3 says this about worldliness and worldly wisdom:

> Who is wise and understanding among you? Let him show it [at Christmas] by his good life, by deeds done in the humility that comes from wisdom. But if you harbor bitter envy and selfish ambition in your hearts, do not boast about it or deny the truth. Such "wisdom" does not come down from heaven but is earthly, unspiritual, of the devil. For where you have envy and selfish ambition, there you find disorder and every evil practice. But the wisdom that comes from heaven

is first of all pure; then peace-loving, considerate, submissive, full of mercy and good fruit, impartial and sincere. (James 3:13–17)

Colossians 3:5 says this about idolatry: "Put to death [at Christmas], therefore, whatever belongs to your earthly nature: immorality, impurity, lust, evil desires and greed, which is idolatry." An idol is anything we put before the Lord in our lives, including our expectations of Christmas *if* we put them ahead of the Lord's expectations of Christmas. What do you do or what do you plan to do to honor, celebrate, and share Jesus on His birthday this year?

> *Lord, help us to celebrate eternal life every day of*
> *the year as we give Christmas back to You. Lord,*
> *may every day be a celebration for Your glory.*
> *Amen*

DAY 22

The Gift of Love

Anyone who does not love does not know God, because God is love. In this the love of God was made manifest among us, that God sent his only Son into the world, so that we might live through him. In this is love, not that we have loved God but that he loved us and sent his Son to be the propitiation for our sins. Beloved, if God so loved us, we also ought to love one another. No one has ever seen God; if we love one another, God abides in us and his love is perfected in us.

—1 John 4:8–12 (esv)

The fourth week of Advent is about being reminded of God's gift of love. Therefore, this fourth week of the Christmas season must also serve as a reminder of God's love. It can be summed up in one name: the name of Jesus. We could rightly say that the last week of Christmas is all about sharing the love of Jesus Christ, the Gospel. God is love (1 John 4:8). Knowing the love of God will have a daily life-changing impact on those who are truly His.

What is the love of God? There are many passages in God's Word that clarify God's love, but probably the most well-known verse is John 3:16: "For God so loved the world, that he gave his only Son, that whoever believes in him should not perish but have eternal life." This verse reminds us this Christmas season that one way God's love is defined is through the act of sacrificial giving. The gift that God gave was not a mere Christmas present. God sacrificially gave His only Son so that whosoever places their faith in His Son, Jesus, would spend an eternity with Him. God's amazing love allows us to either choose or reject God. He loves us so much that He did not force us to receive His gift, but instead, He gave us the choice. Of course, this choice has eternal consequences because through His Son, God mends the separation that sin has caused between Him and us. "But God shows His love for us in that while we were still sinners, Christ died for us" (Rom. 5:8, ESV). God's love was demonstrated with an intense personal sacrifice, and all you and I have to do is accept His gift.

Once we have received God's gift of love, we must share His gift. Jesus reminded us of this in Luke 10:27: "You shall love the Lord your God with all your heart and with all your soul and with all your strength and with all your mind, and your neighbor as yourself." The only way we can truly love anyone else is by sharing with them the love of God. In John 3:16, we find no conditions placed on God's love for us. So if God's love has taken over our life, how can we place conditions on loving others? The answer is, we can't! God doesn't say, "As soon as you clean up your act, I'll love you." God doesn't say, "I'll sacrifice my Son if you promise to love Me." In fact, Romans 5:8 says just the opposite. This Christmas season, God wants us to know that His love is unconditional. God sent His Son, Jesus, to die for us though we did not deserve to be loved. In all reality, God gave us His Son while we were still His enemy and while we were still unlovable. We don't have to clean up our act first. No, by truly receiving God's gift, He makes us clean. I praise God that we don't have to make any promises to Him before we can experience His love. God's love for us has always existed. Therefore, He did all the giving and sacrificing long before we were aware that we even needed His love. Are you sharing God's love with everyone this Christmas season? Remember before you answer this question; His love is unconditional. Therefore, anything other than unconditional love is not love at all.

Lord, help us to truly receive Your perfect gift and love
the way You love. Lord, remind us to share Your love
by giving sacrificially the way that You do. Amen.

DAY 23

A Christmas Prayer

And so, from the day we heard, we have not ceased to pray
for you, asking that you may be filled with the knowledge
of his will in all spiritual wisdom and understanding, so
as to walk in a manner worthy of the Lord, fully pleasing
to him, bearing fruit in every good work and increasing in
the knowledge of God. May you be strengthened with all
power, according to his glorious might, for all endurance
and patience with joy, giving thanks to the Father, who has
qualified you to share in the inheritance of the saints in light.

—Colossians 1:9–12

Paul wanted the Colossian church to know that from the
first day that he heard about their faith, he has prayed for
them without ceasing. Isn't that awesome? That is my aim
for all who are reading this book. I want you all to know

that I continue to pray for you daily. Not that my prayers are any different than yours, but it is comforting to know that people are praying. God led me to share a formula for prayer with you because it is not only how I am praying for you, but it is how you should pray for other believers. Prayer keeps us lifted up, held up, and built up. We all need that, don't we? First, Paul prayed for them all the time. Then he prays they might be "filled with the knowledge of God's will in all spiritual wisdom and understanding." He wanted his brothers and sisters in the faith not only to know God's will, but to understand it and be wise enough to stay in it and live in it. He knew that if they did, then they would "walk in a worthy manner." In other words, they would be living life God's way, and the result would be pleasing God with every step. As believers, we are to live a life that fulfills God's purposes and His will. We were not saved to serve ourselves, but instead, we were saved to serve God alone. Anything less than "walking in the will of God" is undistinguishable from the world and dead ends in disobedience. Being obedient is the key to living right in the center of the will of God. Paul said in Romans 16:19, "Everyone has heard about your obedience." Someone once said, "Obedience is the badge of a person walking closely with God." Paul then prayed that they would be pleasing to God, or in our language, that they might be successful in God's eyes. It has always been God's plan that we be successful. Jeremiah 29:11 says, "For I know the plans I have for you, plans to prosper you and not to harm you, plans to give you hope and a future." This success is not seen by the world nor is it evidenced by our checkbooks, our salaries, the cars we drive, or the homes we live in. No, godly success is spiritual success. How do we know pleasing or successful in God's eyes? Paul said because they will be "bearing fruit in every good work and increasing in our knowledge of God." The same is true for us today. Jesus said, "My true disciples produce much fruit. This brings great glory to my Father" (John 15:8). Jesus also said, "By their fruits you will know them" (Matt. 7:20). What fruit do we bear? Galatians 5:22–23 says, "But the fruit of the Spirit is love, joy, peace, longsuffering, gentleness, goodness, faith, meekness, and temperance: against such there is no law." Our fruit should bear good works and service to others (Titus 3:14). Bearing fruit and increasing in the knowledge of God go hand in hand. The better we get to know Him, the better we trust Him; the better we trust Him, the better we live for Him. So when we are bearing fruit and increasing in our knowledge of God, then we will know that we have found success God's way. By the way, the only source for bearing fruit is the Holy Spirit. We can't manufacture it, so we must plug in to the power source, the Holy Spirit. That is the power Paul prayed for. Finally, Paul prayed for that they have a right attitude. The right attitude for the believer is an attitude of "endurance and patience with joy, thankfulness." This will affect every area of our life and the lives of everyone we come into contact with. The right attitude protects us, allows us to receive God's intervention in our lives, and changes us from the inside out. This is lasting change. This is the change that allows God to filter out our old human nature with the Truth and make us a new creation.

This is my Christmas prayer for you: That you may be filled with the knowledge of His will in all spiritual wisdom and understanding, so as to walk in a manner worthy of the Lord, fully pleasing to Him, bearing fruit in every good work and increasing in the knowledge of God. May you be strengthened with all power, according to His glorious might, for all endurance and patience with joy, giving thanks to the Father. Amen!

The Night before Christmas

> In the beginning was the Word, and the Word was with God, and the Word was God. He was in the beginning with God. All things were made through him, and without him was not anything made that was made. In him was life, and the life was the light of men. The light shines in the darkness, and the darkness has not overcome it.
>
> —John 1:1–5 (ESV)

As we prepare to celebrate the birth of the Savior, it is vital to understand who He was the night before Christmas and who He is today. John 1 gives us this clarity. We find that Jesus the coming Savior is the Creator God. He is personal and real, and He actually dwelt and dwells among us. Knowing who He is much more than some academic intellect. Knowing is a matter of the heart. Knowing Jesus as the Creator is the very first step in salvation. Knowing Him personally is His intent as we find new life in Him. In John 20:31, the writer clarifies the reason it is important that we understand this fact personally as he says, "But these are written so that you may believe that Jesus is the Christ, the Son of God, and that by believing you may have life in his name." The Savior, Jesus, is introduced to us in verse 1 as the Word. Jesus is the Word that spoke most everything into existence, except for you and me. Instead, He loved us so much that He carefully made us with His hands and breathed life into us. When we discover that Jesus is the Creator God, that we can only have life in Him, then that knowledge finds its place in our heart and changes the way we live. Jesus is also the Divine Word. John says, "in the beginning was the Word…" This is a clear reference to Genesis 1:1. When we realize that Jesus existed before creation and therefore existed before His birth on Christmas morn, we conclude that Jesus is coeternal with the Father and therefore uncreated. In fact, Jesus has always been and continuously will be in existence. Colossians 1:15–16 says, "He is the image of the invisible God, the firstborn of all creation. For by him all things were created, in heaven and on earth, visible and invisible, whether thrones or dominions or rulers or authorities—all things were created through him and for him." Jesus the Creator, the Divine Word, took on human flesh that Christmas morning as He was born to Mary and Joseph. As we read a little further in John 1, we find in verses 16–17 that "from His fullness we have all received, grace upon grace…grace and truth came through Jesus Christ." This is the whole reason Jesus came! As we celebrate Christmas this season, we do not celebrate the birth of a tiny little baby. We celebrate the grace, mercy, forgiveness, and truth that the Savior and Creator will bring to us this Christmas. Jesus is God, the Savior, the Creator, the Word, the Way, the Truth, the Life, the Answer for every need in life, and He is the perfect and eternal gift for Christmas.

> *Lord, as we anticipate Christmas this year help us to trust You for Who and all that You are, Amen.*

DAY 24

Resting in Love

Love suffers long, and is kind; love does not envy; love does not parade itself, is not puffed up; does not behave rudely, does not seek its own, is not provoked, thinks no evil; does not rejoice in iniquity, but rejoices in the truth; bears all things, believes all things, hopes all things, endures all things.

—1 Corinthians 13:4–7

If I speak in the tongues of men and of angels, but have not love, I am a noisy gong or a clanging cymbal. And if I have prophetic powers, and understand all mysteries and all knowledge, and if I have all faith, so as to remove mountains, but have not love, I am nothing. If I give away all I have, and if I deliver up my body to be burned, but have not love, I gain nothing. Love is patient and kind; love does not envy or boast;

it is not arrogant or rude. It does not insist on its own way; it is not irritable or resentful; it does not rejoice at wrongdoing, but rejoices with the truth. Love bears all things, believes all things, hopes all things, endures all things. Love never ends. As for prophecies, they will pass away; as for tongues, they will cease; as for knowledge, it will pass away. For we know in part and we prophesy in part, but when the perfect comes, the partial will pass away. When I was a child, I spoke like a child, I thought like a child, I reasoned like a child. When I became a man, I gave up childish ways. For now we see in a mirror dimly, but then face to face. Now I know in part; then I shall know fully, even as I have been fully known. So now faith, hope, and love abide, these three; but the greatest of these is love.

—1 Corinthians 13 (esv)

There is one more day in our twenty-five days of Christmas. It seems as though time has flown by. Just a reminder, this last week of Advent or the Christmas season is to be all about God's love. So, we have talked about one standout quality of God's love so far. We have talked about the fact that God's love is unconditional. God's love is the standard and the source for the love that flows within and out of us. God's love is not based on feelings or emotions. God doesn't stop loving us because we're unlovable or only love us when we make Him feel good. No, God loves us because He is love.

Love is also a sacrificial gift. True love always loves even when it takes sacrifice to do so. In fact, Jesus said "no greater love has any man than to lay down his life for another." And because God is love, He created you and me for a loving relationship with Him. And even though our sin separated us from the possibility of that relationship God willingly sacrificed His own Son to restore that relationship. "Oh, how He loves us!"

There have been so many hymns and songs written to help paint a picture of God's love for us, but none paints this picture better in my heart than "The Love of God" by Frederick M. Lehman.

> The love of God is greater far
> Than tongue or pen can ever tell;
> It goes beyond the highest star,
> And reaches to the lowest hell;
> The guilty pair, bowed down with care,
> God gave His Son to win;
> His erring child He reconciled,
> And pardoned from his sin.
>
> Refrain:
> Oh, love of God, how rich and pure!
> How measureless and strong!
> It shall forevermore endure—
> The saints' and angels' song.
> When hoary time shall pass away,
> And earthly thrones and kingdoms fall,
> When men who here refuse to pray,

> On rocks and hills and mountains call,
> God's love so sure, shall still endure,
> All measureless and strong;
> Redeeming grace to Adam's race—
> The saints' and angels' song.
> Could we with ink the ocean fill,
> And were the skies of parchment made,
> Were every stalk on earth a quill,
> And every man a scribe by trade;
> To write the love of God above,
> Would drain the ocean dry;
> Nor could the scroll contain the whole,
> Though stretched from sky to sky.

So many things can be said and songs sung about the love of God, but it would take an eternity to say or sing them all. God's eternal love is vital to sustaining life, and sharing His love is vital to our spiritual growth. In fact, someone once said, "Love is the measure of our faith, the inspiration for our obedience, and the true altitude of our discipleship."

The Holy Spirit through the apostle Paul did an amazing job penning the description of God's love and reminding us that we are nothing without His love. Let's talk about the first seven verses of 1 Corinthians 13. Verses 1–3 remind us that God's love is the necessity to living for Him:

> Though I speak with the tongues of men and of angels, but have not love, I have become sounding brass or a clanging cymbal. And though I have the

gift of prophecy, and understand all mysteries and all knowledge, and though I have all faith, so that I could remove mountains, but have not love, I am nothing. And though I bestow all my goods to feed the poor, and though I give my body to be burned, but have not love, it profits me nothing.

In verses 4–7, we find God's description of His love.

Love suffers long, and is kind; love does not envy; love does not parade itself, is not puffed up; does not behave rudely, does not seek its own, is not provoked, thinks no evil; does not rejoice in iniquity, but rejoices in the truth; bears all things, believes all things, hopes all things, endures all things.

Oh, listen, God is love; therefore, when we read these verses, we can adequately substitute God's name for *love* anytime. So we can rightly read that "God suffers long and is kind...," and because He lives in us, we can rightly place our name in each verse for *love* to see if we are truly reflecting Jesus or God's love or not. We must make it personal because it is!

Lord, help us to always rest in Your love by sharing Your love. Lord, may we never just be a bunch of noise when it comes to reflecting Your Son. Lord, help us to take this relationship with You and make it more personal than anything else. Lord, may we bring You the honor and glory that You are due this Christmas season. Amen.

The Arrival of the Savior

If I speak in the tongues of men and of angels, but have not love, I am a noisy gong or a clanging cymbal. And if I have prophetic powers, and understand all mysteries and all knowledge, and if I have all faith, so as to remove mountains, but have not love, I am nothing. If I give away all I have, and if I deliver up my body to be burned, but have not love, I gain nothing. Love is patient and kind; love does not envy or boast; it is not arrogant or rude. It does not insist on its own way; it is not irritable or resentful; it does not rejoice at wrongdoing, but rejoices with the truth. Love bears all things, believes all things, hopes all things, endures all things. Love never ends. As for prophecies, they will pass away; as for tongues, they will cease; as for knowledge, it will pass away. For we know in part and we prophesy in part, but when the perfect comes, the partial will pass away. When

> I was a child, I spoke like a child, I thought like a child,
> I reasoned like a child. When I became a man, I gave up
> childish ways. For now we see in a mirror dimly, but then
> face to face. Now I know in part; then I shall know fully,
> even as I have been fully known. So now faith, hope, and
> love abide, these three; but the greatest of these is love.
>
> —1 Corinthians 13:1–13 (esv)

Here we are, day twenty-five of the Christmas season and Christmas Eve. What an amazing journey it has been as our travels this season led us to be prepared for the coming of Christ, to live in and share the hope of Christ, to be filed with and share the good news of great joy, and in the final week of Advent or the Christmas season, we are learning that we are to dwell in and share the love of God.

Yesterday, we talked about how the first seven verses of 1 Corinthians 13. We found that these seven verses more than adequately describe God's love and remind us that we are nothing without His love. We talked about the fact that God is love, and because He is, then as we read 1 Corinthians 13, we can adequately substitute God's name for *love* every time gaining an amazing picture of who He is, and because He lives in us, we can rightly replace the word *love* with our name to see if we are truly reflecting Jesus or God's love. When we do, we find that we must make God's love personal, because it is!

The remainder of 1 Corinthians 13 talks about the supremacy of God and His love with phrases like, "Love never fails." God's love will never fail us. He demonstrated this when "He so loved the world that He gave His only begotten Son that whosoever believes in Him will not perish, but instead will inherit eternal life." The first Christmas is a reminder that God loved us so much that He took on flesh, as He was born of a virgin, came to save us from sin, and restored our relationship with the Father. God loved us enough to send His Son, Emmanuel (meaning "God with us"), so that we might know firsthand that He will never leave us nor forsake us. Oh, listen, Jesus is the Messiah and Redeemer that gave us the gift of salvation as He died on the cross, paying the wages of our sin. He is the El Shaddai (Lord God Almighty), Creator, and El Olam (the Everlasting One) who defeated the grave and death at His resurrection to give us the gift of eternal life, and He is God on High, Elohim (Sovereign God), and Jehovah or Yahweh who will return to usher His own into eternity with Him (heaven) and judge those who knew Him not, sending them to be eternally separated from Him (hell).

When we recognize the supremacy of God, we realize that investing in anything else is futile. He is the only investment with eternal returns. Verse 13 reminds us of the ways God invests in us, and we are to invest in Him: "So now faith, hope, and love abide, these three; but the greatest of these is love." When we see God, both faith and hope will be realized and deemed worth investing our lives in. We have been justified by faith, we rejoice in hope, but love (God's love) is the greater than them all. Love is the true gift and the true investment that trumps all things. Why? Because when you give love, you give God, and when you get love, you get God. Will you give the greatest Christmas ever this year?

Lord, help use to recognize Your supremacy, and as we do, help us to invest solely in You. Lord, may we always be givers of the greatest gift, Your love (Jesus). Amen.

Christmas Is the Day a Baby Changed Everything

From Isaiah 9

For unto us a child is born, unto us a son is given; and the government shall be upon his shoulder; and his name shall be called Wonderful, Counselor, The Mighty God, The Everlasting Father; the Prince of Peace.

Of the increase of his government and peace there shall be no end, upon the throne of David, and upon his kingdom, to order it, and to establish it with judgment and with justice from hence-forth even for ever.

From Matthew 1

Now the birth of Jesus Christ was on this wise: When as his mother Mary was espoused to Joseph, before they came together, she was found with child of the Holy Ghost.

Then Joseph her husband, being a just man and not willing to make a public example, was minded to put her away privily.

But while he thought on these things, behold the angel of the Lord appeared unto him in a dream, saying "Joseph, thou son of David, fear not to take unto thee Mary, thy wife; for that which is conceived in her is of the Holy Ghost.

"And she shall bring forth a son, and thou shalt call his name JESUS; for he shall save his people from their sins."

From Luke 2

And it came to pass in those days, that there went out a decree from Caesar Augustus, that all the world should be taxed. (And this taxing was first made when Cyrenius was governor of Syria.) And all went to be taxed, every one into his own city.

And Joseph also went up from Galilee, out of the city of Nazareth, into Judea, unto the city of David, which is called Bethlehem; (because he was of the house and lineage of David;) To be taxed with Mary his espoused wife, being great with child.

And so it was, that, while they were there the days were accomplished that she should be delivered. And she brought forth her firstborn son, and wrapped him in swaddling clothes, and laid him in a manger; because there was no room for them in the inn.

And there were in the same country shepherds abiding in the field, keeping watch over their flock by night. And, lo, the angel of the Lord came unto them; and the glory of the Lord shone round about them, and they were sore afraid.

And the angel said unto them, "Fear not, for, behold, I bring you good tidings of great joy, which shall be to all people. For unto you is born this day in the city of David a Savior, which is Christ the Lord. And this shall be a sign unto you: Ye shall find the babe wrapped in swaddling clothes, lying in a manger."

And suddenly there was with the angel a multitude of the heavenly host praising God and saying, "Glory to God in the highest, and on earth peace, good will toward men."

And it came to pass, as the angels were gone away from them into heaven, the shepherds said one to another, "Let us now go even unto Bethlehem, and see this thing which is come to pass, which the Lord hath made known unto us." And they came with haste, and found Mary, and Joseph, and the babe lying in a manger.

Then Arrived the Original Christmas Missionaries

And in the same region there were shepherds out in the field, keeping watch over their flock by night. And an angel of the Lord appeared to them, and the glory of the Lord shone around them, and they were filled with great fear. And the angel said to them, "Fear not, for behold, I bring you good news of great joy that will be for all the people. For unto you is born this day in the city of David a Savior, who is Christ the Lord. And this will be a sign for you: you will find a baby wrapped in swaddling cloths and lying in a manger." And suddenly there was with the angel a multitude of the heavenly host praising God and saying, "Glory to God in the highest, and on earth peace among those with whom he is pleased!" When the angels went away from them into heaven, the shepherds said to one another, "Let us go over to Bethlehem and see this thing that has happened, which the Lord has made known to us." And they went with haste and found Mary and Joseph, and the baby lying in a manger. And when they saw it, they made known the saying that had

been told them concerning this child. And all who heard
it wondered at what the shepherds told them. But Mary
treasured up all these things, pondering them in her heart.
And the shepherds returned, glorifying and praising God
for all they had heard and seen, as it had been told them.

—Luke 2:8–20 (esv)

While the prophets may have told a story about one who
would come, the shepherds would first proclaim the one…
who had come.

As followers of Christ, we should do nothing less this
Christmas season than be Christmas missionaries. We should
be telling others the story of the good news…of Christ who
has come to all of us. There is no better time for us doing
this than in this season in which we especially celebrate the
Savior's birth.

Notice these first Christmas missionaries received a declaration.
Verses 10–14 say,

But the angel said to them, "Do not be afraid. I bring
you good news of great joy that will be for all the
people. Today in the town of David a Savior has been
born to you; he is Christ the Lord. This will be a sign
to you: You will find a baby wrapped in cloths and
lying in a manger." Suddenly a great company of the
heavenly host appeared with the angel, praising God
and saying, "Glory to God in the highest, and on earth
peace to men on whom his favor rests."

It was the declaration of *good news*.
The shepherds were then filled with anticipation.

Look closely at verse 15 (emphasis added) and feel the excitement of the shepherds come alive as they experience anticipation in their heart. This is the same excitement that we should feel this Christmas morning. "When the angels had left them and gone into heaven, the shepherds said to one another, *'Let's go!'*" Does the birth of the Savior cause you to excitedly go around sharing the good news? It should! There was absolutely no hesitation on their part. Verses 15–16 say, "Let's go to Bethlehem and see this thing that has happened, which the Lord has told us about. So they hurried off and found Mary and Joseph, and the baby, who was lying in the manger."

The Christmas message is

> *A message of good news*
> *A message of joy*
> *A message that would bring hope for all people*

We have received the same message! If we have received this same declaration, then where is our anticipation? Where is our excitement? An excitement not only over a Savior who has come, but a Savior who is *coming again as King!* We ought to be Christmas missionaries taking the declaration we have heard and received, with great anticipation, and we should be hurrying to tell others the message. When we do this, just as the shepherds did that very first Christmas night, there will be *declaration*.

Not only did those shepherds go and see but also then, they went and told.

Those first Christmas missionaries, the shepherds, got involved sharing that declaration which actually begins as an activity of decoration.

The shepherds began an activity of decoration.

Verse 17 says, "When they had seen [Jesus], they spread the word concerning what had been told them about this child, they spread the word…" They really began to spread Christmas cheer. They began to *decorate* the lives of those they could share with. As the decoration begins, it is as if they were turning on beautiful Christmas lights with each person that the shepherds told. Verses 18–19 say, "And all who heard it were amazed at what the shepherds said to them. But Mary treasured up all these things and pondered them in her heart." They shepherds went about decorating Christmas wherever they went. How did they decorate this first Christmas, you might ask? Not with tinsel or garland. Not with glass, balls, or glowing lights, but they spread the word of God's light, which had come into the world.

They decorated the world with God's love! How are we decorating this Christmas? Are we decorating the lives of all those we can with the light of God's love…by spreading the Word. Decoration is that which beautifies. There is nothing that beautifies the world more than God's marvelous love made known to all people throughout your community and then throughout the earth. Decorating with the message of God's having sent a Savior into the world. When the shepherds went out telling the good news of a Savior who was born, it caused people's lives to light up like a beautiful ornament. Verse 19 says, "All who heard it were amazed at what the shepherds said to them."

The decoration made a difference in the shepherds' life.

Verse 20 says, "The shepherds returned, glorifying and praising God for all the things they had heard and seen, which were just as they had been told." Sure, these shepherds returned to their fields, but they returned different. They returned changed. Before Christmas, the shepherds' conversations were probably about how many stars there were in the sky, but now they were filled with conversation of the One Star of heaven and earth that shined bright with a promise for all. Their lives became fountains of glory and praise to God who had brought them salvation. They were not only living; they were a living testimony of a changed life. A life now dedicated to the one thing that really made a difference. How is it with you and me?

We have heard the declaration, so where is our anticipation? How are we decorating the world? Are we decorating it with God's love by the sharing Jesus Christ and spreading the *good news*? Are we demonstrating that changed life? A life of dedication and a life that is praising and glorifying God just as those first Christmas missionaries did? This Christmas, we have a special opportunity to take the *declaration* we have received and to go out and get involved with *decorating* by spreading the good news to others. Let us never grow weary in our changed life of *dedication* to praising and glorifying God.

It Is Time to Celebrate!

Every valley shall be filled in, every mountain and hill made low. The crooked roads shall become straight, the rough ways smooth. And all mankind will see God's salvation.

—Luke 3:5–6

Our Lord fills in the valleys of despair in our hearts. It is God who is able to make molehills out of our mountains. Jesus creates straight roads out of our crooked paths of disobedience. Our Savior makes our rough hearts smooth with his precious blood. John says, "Prepare." Thankfully, God is the one who prepares us. It is the Holy Spirit who opens our ears to hear so that our hearts that they may believe.

Our eternal salvation is so important that our gracious God would not let this depend on our choice or decision. It is by grace we have been saved not by our works, not by our desire, but by God's grace alone. Ezekiel 11:19 says, "I will give them an undivided heart and put a new spirit in them; I will remove from them their heart of stone and give them a heart of flesh." Our stone-cold, hardened hearts have been graciously changed into hearts of flesh.

This can only happen by the power and miracle of God's grace. In our hearts, our loving Lord plants the seed of His Word so that it may bear abundant fruit. Listen to another Old Testament messenger. Jeremiah 24:7 states, "I will give them a heart to know me, that I am the LORD. They will be my people, and I will be their God, for they will return to me with all their heart."

By God's grace, we need to be preparing our hearts to celebrate Christmas—not just our homes. The Lord has given us hearts to know him and to love him as His children. Not just for a day but for eternity. Malachi's message about John the Baptist was clear. John's message prepared men's hearts for Jesus. Jesus, the messenger of the covenant, the one they desired would come to His temple. Jesus would refine and purify worship. Remember when Jesus drove out the money changers because the temple was to be His Father's house of worship? Jesus had warned the Pharisees and leaders, but worship during Jesus's time had become a duty, a sense of obligation and not praise. For generations, the people brought sacrifices. They had forgotten why they worship and now did as they were ordered. The leaders demanded; the people obeyed. They grew indifferent to worship's true meaning.

Jesus taught that worship was a matter of the heart—love, not an outward show or duty. We might be tempted to point at the people during the time of Malachi. How could they become so indifferent? We might point to the leaders and worshippers of Jesus's day. How did they become so indifferent? They sinned. We sin.

We might also take our faith for granted from time to time. It can be so easy to be caught up in the commercialism of our society rather than the true spirit of worshipping the Christ-child.

We daily fall short of the glory of God. Daniel 11:35 says, "Some of the wise will stumble, so that they may be refined, purified and made spotless until the time of the end, for it will still come at the appointed time."

Our gracious God uses His word and His Spirit to refine and purify us. After recognizing our sinfulness, the Gospel of Jesus Christ makes us spotless. Jesus's death and resurrection purifies sinners. We see our sins. We confess our sins. We trust in God's mercy. Our sins are forgiven. All is right with the world. Or is it? Our world is still infected with sin. This means that on this side of heaven there is not one thing in life that is perfect. We face difficulties, heartaches, sorrows, and troubles every day.

All these things are not meant to overcome us. Instead, God uses everything every day in our lives to purify us— make our faith stronger.

James 1:2–3 says, "Consider it pure joy, my brothers, whenever you face trials of many kinds, because you know that the testing of your faith develops perseverance." When we are weak, God is our strength. When we are sad, God is our comfort. In our sinfulness, God is forgiving. Purifying has the implication of refining. Facing the events in our lives refines our faith. *Purify* also means to make clean or holy. On our own, we are lost and condemned. On our own, we are unclean and unholy.

Again, through faith by God's grace, all that has been changed for us. First John 1:7 reminds us "if we walk in the light, as he is in the light, we have fellowship with one another, and the blood of Jesus, his Son, purifies us from all sin." God's Son, Jesus, our Savior, purifies us from *all* sin!

In conclusion, there is great excitement and expectation as we prepare to celebrate Jesus's birth, but we also need to celebrate that Jesus will come again, not as a baby but as the King of Kings and the Lord of Lords.

We often say love came down at Christmas. Jesus' coming is God's way of telling us how much He loves us. In Malachi's day, there were many people who ignored the truth. Malachi 2:17 even records people who said then what some say now that "all who do evil are good in the eyes of the Lord and He is pleased with them." Nothing could be further from the truth.

God's love did come down at Christmas, but God does not delight in seeing the wicked go by unpunished. Nor does God like to see the innocent condemned (Prov. 17:13, NIV; paraphrased). Therefore, we can hope. Hope is why Love came down at Christmas.

This time of year is a special season, a season when we should open our hearts and our minds for our Savior to dwell in our hearts and lives. So that we can keep hoping, looking ahead, and keep looking up. God has sent His messengers, and God continues to send His messengers to prepare the way. As sinners made holy by the blood of Christ, we are now supposed to be the ones preparing the way for Jesus return.

The Lord is coming (Mal. 3:1). The world was obviously not ready when Jesus came the first time. There was no room for Jesus in the inn. Jesus is the King, and kings are supposed to be treated as royalty and with respect. Jesus had no crib for a bed. Certainly, a King deserves the finest bed around. A King deserves the best, but Jesus was placed in a manger...a feeding trough...a place where animals eat. That is no place for a baby. It is no place for a King. It certainly is no place for Jesus!

The world was not ready when Jesus came the first time. You would think that the innkeeper would have at least asked for someone to give up their room for this woman who was pregnant with child. At least a room would have had four walls and a roof. Was this the best that the world could do for the King? Was this the best the world could do to welcome the Lord? The star in the sky should have been a clue that Jesus was no ordinary baby, but no one was looking up toward God.

At least the wise men were not too blind to look up. This star was God's birth announcement to the world that the Savior had been born. How do we respond today to God's love coming down to us at Christmas through Jesus? God wants us to respond by returning to Him. God knows that we cannot come to Him without His help. That is why love came down at Christmas through Jesus. The manger of Bethlehem cradles a King...a Savior. He is God with us, our Emmanuel. The Lord has come to save us from our sins. Jesus has come saying return to Him in righteousness...the righteousness that He Himself provides for us by shedding His blood on the cross...by rising from the grave and defeating death. There probably has been no greater need than in the present time for those who have Christ in their hearts and lives to share that blessing with those still in darkness.

Christmas is a time to prepare for the King. Are you prepared for Him? Have you prepares for Him a palace or a stable? A throne or a manger?

> *Lord help us to be prepared like never before by allowing You to clean our stable and make it a palace, and by giving You the through throne of our lives insisting you lay in a manger. In Jesus's Mighty Name, Amen.*

Bibliography

Johnson Oatman, Jr., pub.1897 "Count Your Blessings."

Crossway Bibles. 2007. ESV: Sstudy Bible : English Sstandard Vversion. ESV Text ed. Wheaton, Ill: Crossway Bibles, 2007.

Holy Bible: New Living Translation. Wheaton, IL: Tyndale House, 1996.

Nelson's Ulimate Bible Reference Library. Thomas Nelson, Inc. 2008.

Holy Bible: New International Version. Grand Rapids, MI: Zondervan, 1978. Logos

Bible Software. Vers.3. CD-ROM. Libronix, 2000–2006.

The Holy Bible, King James Version. New York: American Bible Society: 1999; Bartleby.com, 2000. www.bartleby.com/108/